EARL WARREN
Governor of California

Books by Richard B. Harvey

The Dynamics of California Politics and Government

Earl Warren: Governor of California

EARL WARREN

Governor of California

Richard B. Harvey

Whittier College

An Exposition-University Book
EXPOSITION PRESS   **New York**

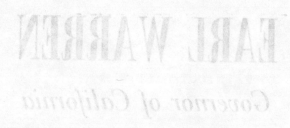

EXPOSITION PRESS INC.

50 Jericho Turnpike   Jericho, N. Y. 11753

FIRST EDITION

LIBRARY OF CONGRESS CATALOG CARD NUMBER: 69-17230

EP 46920

TO PAT, SCOTT AND TIM

TO PAT, SCOTT AND TIM

Preface

Earl Warren held the governorship of California from January 4, 1943, to October 5, 1953, nearly eleven years. His service in that office, though technically under Republican auspices, was characterized by a distinct nonpartisan flavor and reflected a progressive stance not ordinarily thought of as in keeping with traditional Republicanism. There exists a general popular recollection of Warren as fitting that pattern; however, little analysis has been made of the nature and techniques of his political approach prior to his departure for Washington to become chief justice of the United States. This book is an attempt to meet that shortcoming, and secondarily to relate his political practices and principles to his behavior on the Supreme Court.

I wish to extend my warmest thanks to the Haynes Foundation and to Whittier College, both of which materially aided this study through the provision and tender of a liberal grant. A particular debt of gratitude is owed to Dr. Paul Smith, president of Whittier College, Dean Roy Newsom, and Dr. J. William Robinson, chairman of the Department of Political Science. I am especially grateful for the help and encouragement generously given by Dr. Ivan Hinderaker, chancellor of the University of California, Riverside, as well as for the editorial and substantive comments of a number of others.

I would be remiss if I failed to acknowledge the splendid co-operation and cordial attention accorded my requests for materials and advice by Dr. Benjamin Whitten and his fine staff of the Whittier College library. The same can be said for many persons at the library of the University of California, Los Angeles, particularly Miss Dorothy Wells in the Institute of Govermental Studies, Miss Hilda Gray, formerly of the Government Publications Room, and Mr. James Mink of the Department of Special

Collections. Mr. James Otley and his assistants in the California Room of the State Library at Sacramento gave courteous consideration to my requests for use of the *Warren Speeches*, newspaper files, and other sources.

To the many authorities who willingly gave of their time and thinking in personal interviews and to those responsible for written works I have cited, I express my sincere appreciation. For the understanding and encouragement given by my wife, Patricia, and my son, Scott, during the often frustrating chore of completing the project, I need hardly express my lasting gratitude. Finally, I should note, I am personally responsible for any errors of fact or judgment that may have crept into the work, an admission not likely to be disputed.

R. B. H.

Contents

Preface   7

List of Tables   11

PART ONE   The Governor as Politician   13

  I   *Earl Warren: Political Practices and Political Principles*   15

The Warren Political Approach in Retrospect 16 / Elements of the Warren Political Approach 18 / The Doctrine of Social Progress 24

PART TWO   Politics, Warren Style: Campaigns, Program Development, and Legislative Relations   29

  II   *Earl Warren: The Political Campaigner*   31

Campaign Organization 32 / Campaign Finance 40 / Campaign Style: Political Independence and Personal Government 46 / Campaign Style: Caution and Emphasis on the Record 57

  III   *Earl Warren: Executive Policymaker*   67

Program Development, Warren Style 68 / The Citizen Advisory Bodies 70 / The Official Family 80 / The Governor's Council 90

  IV   *Earl Warren: Legislative Advocate*   95

The Warren Theme: Legislative Independence 96 /
Legislative Leadership, Warren Style 99 / California's
Legislature: The Debasement of Partisanship 107 / The
Legislature Disposes: The Pattern of Action on the
Warren Programs 111

PART THREE   The Warren Political Style and Public
                   Policy: Health, Welfare, and Labor Issues   117

   V   *Earl Warren: Program Innovator*   119

The Governor and the Health Issue 119 / The Chief
Executive and Social Welfare 132 / Warren and Labor
142

PART FOUR   Earl Warren, the California Governorship,
                   and the Supreme Court   161

   VI   *Earl Warren, Social Progress, and Republicanism*   163

Political Strategy or Fundamental Principle? 163 / Earl
Warren and Party Politics 167

   VII   *Mr. Chief Justice*   175

"Individualism" and "Cooperative Endeavor" in a Judicial Setting 175 / The Judicial Administrator: Pragmatic "Problem Solving" and "Cooperative Endeavor"
on the Supreme Court 183 / Judicial Activism, the Individual, and Constitutional Fundamentals 188 / Social
Progress, Adaptability, and Judicial Activism: The Race
Issue 193 / The Chief Justice and His Critics 197

   Bibliographic Notes   203

List of Tables

Table 1 Some Democratic Participants in 1950 Warren
          Campaign   38
Table 2 Contributions and Expenditures for Warren
          Gubernatorial Campaigns   43
Table 3 Campaign Contributions by California
          Republican Bodies, 1950   45
Table 4 Support (Floor Vote) for Warren Positions
          in California Legislature: Democratic vs.
          Republican   115
Table 5 Support (Floor Vote) for Warren Positions
          in California Legislature: Metropolitan vs.
          Nonmetropolitan   115
Table 6 Support (Floor Vote) for Warren Positions in
          California Legislature: Northern vs. Southern   116

PART ONE

The Governor as Politician

CHAPTER I

Earl Warren: Political Practices and Political Principles

Earl Warren was, to an extent, heir to the legacy left by Hiram Johnson, California's Progressive chief executive from 1911 to 1917. Johnson, an independent in philosophy, although a Republican by registration—at least during most of his public career—presided over a number of enactments which substantially reduced the role played by political parties in California affairs. Included were such measures as the cross-filing system, which permitted candidates for partisan public office to seek nomination from more than the party of their own affiliation and to construct a broad, bipartisan following in the process; alterations in the structure of official party bodies which emasculated their operations; introduction of formal nonpartisanship at local levels of government, which weakened the partisan base for political activities in California; and institution of direct legislation through the initiative and referendum, which tended to separate many leading California issues from the parties per se and to place responsibility for their proposal and advancement largely with interest groups.

Swift population growth made it difficult for parties to build a stable foundation. The diverse sectional character of the Golden State impaired the development of smooth-functioning statewide parties. These factors brought about an eventual proliferation of volunteer party bodies, created a vacuum made to order for the propagation and concerted activity of pressure groups, and resulted in the evolution of political public-relations firms. Most significantly, they gave rise to a political milieu in which a nonpartisan appeal paid handsome dividends.

The Warren Political Approach in Retrospect

Earl Warren has been a Republican all his adult life. He was a party officer, serving as chairman of the state central committee from 1934 to 1936 and as national committeeman from 1936 to 1938. A favorite-son candidate for President in the 1936, 1944, and 1948 primaries, he became Republican nominee for the vice presidency in 1948 and spoke on behalf of the ticket in 1944 and 1952. In 1952 he openly sought his party's presidential nomination.

Nevertheless, Warren attempted to keep partisan functions separate from governmental duties. This was his behavior in his earlier career as Alameda County district attorney from 1925 to 1939, as California attorney general between 1939 and 1943, and during his governorship. In a sense he played two separate and distinct roles—party leader and public servant. The two were not to be mixed. As one authority summed it up: "Warren was a man who could carry water on either shoulder, political or official, but never at the same time."[1]

This desire by Warren to disassociate himself from partisan politics was evident from his conduct in various aspects of the state governmental process. It was exemplified by the type of campaign he undertook for the highest executive office, by the kind of advice he relied upon in formulating his programs, and by the sort of backing he secured in the legislative branch on his recommendations.

Warren carried on his gubernatorial election efforts separately from those of Republicans running for other posts, thus emphasizing personal accountability to the electorate. He formed his own organization and tapped funds largely apart from more partisan sources. In fact, a number of Democrats played prominent roles in his electoral efforts. In his quests for re-election in 1946 and

---

[1] Bernard Brennan, Los Angeles lawyer, Warren campaign manager for Southern California in 1946, and former chairman of the Los Angeles County Republican Central Committee. Interview, Dec. 27, 1956.

1950, Warren criticized the opposition for trying to categorize all GOP candidates as a single group and to place all Democratic hopefuls in a united struggle against them. The Governor rarely endorsed other office seekers of his own political registration and avoided party concerns while campaigning, hoping to make substantive issues and his own record the major points of debate.

Warren also reached across partisan lines to evolve ideas for his legislative agenda. He made extensive use of citizen advisory bodies. Generally these conferences, committees, and commissions were representative of numerous segments of California thought, regardless of partisanship. The Governor did not ordinarily seek counsel from ranking Republican or Democratic party functionaries as such. Their suggestions on any question, if elicited, were valued only as opinions of individuals with some competence to deal with the matter at hand. Most members of his official family were Republicans, although several Democrats occupied state posts at his request. Professionalization of high positions dependent upon his appointment was a prime Warren goal. He wished to attract persons qualified by training and experience in special fields—an ideal that was reflected also in his utilization of lay and expert advisory committees in naming several department directors. Many measures sent to the legislators by Warren were conceived and developed by these agency heads and their career civil service staffs. Others were nurtured through discussions with legislators of both parties.

An absence of partisan appeal was also patent in Warren's relationship with the California legislature. He advocated "mutual respect and separate responsibility" between legislative and executive branches. He did not organize a party group or an intimate Warren clique within either house and he refrained from openly denoting his preferences for leadership in the assembly or the senate. The Governor respected the ability of legislators to comprehend the issues facing California. He tried to formulate statutory objectives in as broad a manner as possible, allowing leeway for the lawmakers to find more definite solutions within the larger goal. The Chief Executive was a devotee of moderate progress in programmatic matters. Given to compromise, he shunned the headstrong, all-or-nothing stance. He preferred open, give-and-take negotiations and influence through frank public relations in persuading the solons to follow certain courses. The record discloses that his legislative policy yielded rather handsome results in terms of bipartisan support.

Warren's divergence from views held by many of his fellow Republicans was especially apparent in his espousal of social legislation, primarily in the fields of health, welfare, and labor. Promotion of such liberal proposals as compulsory health insurance; extensions of social welfare, unemployment, and workmen's compensation benefits; and a fair employment practices measure resembled Democratic pronouncements in these areas. Such items, coupled with a vast construction program on state highways, correctional facilities and mental health facilities—all involving extensive expenditures and a constantly rising budget—did not meet with universal favor in Republican circles. They not only induced a number of legislators of Democratic persuasion to cast their lot with the Governor at different times but were doubtless an important factor in the sizable popular vote he received from the Democratic party in each gubernatorial election. Seeking the Democratic nomination as well as his own in three successful tries for the top California office, Warren captured both party primaries in 1946—the only aspirant for the governorship to do so under the famous state cross-filing system. He ran well enough on the Democratic ticket in both 1942 and 1950 to carry himself to an electoral triumph in November over his rivals. In the three primaries the Democratic votes divided in this manner: in 1942—Warren 404,778, Olson 514,144; in 1946—Warren 593,180, Kenny 530,968; in 1950—Warren 719,468, Roosevelt 969,433.

Elements of the Warren Political Approach

To a considerable extent the political approach of Warren as governor was based upon pure political strategy. The prevailing nonpartisan atmosphere furnished a background for capture of public office by those willing to minimize party allegiance. The

Democrats acquired a registration advantage beginning in 1934 and their numerical supremacy reached tremendous proportions at the peak of Warren's career. As an astute politician he naturally hoped to make the best of this potentially unfortunate situation. His formula was simple: by de-emphasizing Republican ties and promising nonpartisanship in managing state affairs, as well as by recommending liberal social measures, he sought to attract sufficient Democratic voters to forge a winning coalition. That strategy was highly profitable.

Warren also assumed, and apparently with good reason, that most rank-and-file Republicans would favor that type of political approach. The average California Republican likewise had comparatively lax party attachments and could be expected to agree more readily with such behavior than his fellow partisans in many other parts of the United States. It could be appreciated as an electoral weapon with which to subdue the rival Democrats, if for no other reason. As time passed, those in the GOP of more conservative and partisan bent had little alternative but to accept Warren as state chief executive. Nor was Warren's brand of politics limited in its fortunate results to the popular ballot. It also worked well in luring Democratic legislators to his side, particularly on social issues in the fields of health, welfare, and labor.

The Governor's tendency to play down party loyalty was not solely a matter of expediency. His personality was every bit as salient a factor. Temperamentally ill-suited for heated partisanship, moderate by nature, he tried not to arouse personal antagonisms, even in dealing with political adversaries. A man of pragmatic mentality not given to deep intellectual searching or abstraction, Warren invariably told his subordinates and associates that he must have "the facts" before acting on any question. The facts sometimes led him along lines unorthodox for a Republican.

His practical inclination gave Warren a healthy respect for political realities. Success through accentuating a nonpartisan theme as candidate for attorney general in 1938 was a lesson for later years. Democrat Robert W. Kenny, who endorsed Warren that year and succeeded him in the office in 1943, said: "Warren was our first real 'serendipidist' in California politics, one who has the faculty of making happy and unexpected discoveries by accident."[2] Moveover, some of Warren's earlier experiences gave him the impressions for subsequent state programs. To Kenny, whom he defeated for governor in 1946, Warren related how his illness and hospitalization in 1944, coupled with difficulties over his insurance policy, caused him to reflect further upon medical costs for ordinary citizens. As Alameda County district attorney he had prosecuted a fraudulent health-insurance ring.

Warren's prior professional life aided in shaping him for the position of California chief executive. As a law-enforcement officer for many years, he was accustomed to service in a non-partisan office. This was probably a boon to his initial gubernatorial candidacy in 1942, when wartime simplified the task of an aspirant with that background. From the GOP viewpoint, a nominee with such a record also improved the party's own chances for capitalizing upon prevailing sentiments for unity. Warren took advantage of this set of facts. He continued, however, to abide by his nonpartisan stance for the rest of his tenure, undoubtedly to the chagrin of some ardent Republicans.

Elements of political strategy and personality aside, Warren also held certain convictions that guided his conduct of the California governorship. Believing that accomplishment was based upon cooperative endeavor, he conceived his responsibility to be the creation of a climate in which citizens could collaborate harmoniously in attacking state problems. His feeling of "partnership" with the general public was mirrored in his concept of the role of government. Resorting to a football analogy, the Governor rejected both the conservative notion that political authorities should be simply neutral arbiters on the field and the radical idea that they were the captain, quarterback, other principal players, and officials combined. Rather, public representatives were in the contest but certainly were not the whole team. In his

---

[2] Robert W. Kenny (D), judge of the Superior Court of Los Angeles County, former attorney general of California, 1943-47, defeated by Warren for governor in 1946. Interview, Dec. 27, 1957.

words: "It is my belief that government is, in fact, the people engaged in one phase of their total activity, and that government therefore cannot remain aloof from, or disinterested in, the game in which we seek to reach our goals."[3]

His post-World War II building program illustrated this idea. Such public works projects were intended to furnish additional employment opportunities for a growing number of residents at a time when industry was readjusting to normal production, aside from improvements in state facilities. In 1943 Warren observed: "No single agency or group can guarantee a satisfactory return to peacetime conditions. The best approach will always lie in a broad and cooperative attack by private industry, business organizations, and enterprising individuals, assisted by the agencies of government . . . Private enterprise must always have the right of way in creating jobs, and in back of private enterprise the government should stand ready to help whenever it can."[4]

It probably was inevitable that a feeling of affinity with the people would induce the Governor to report conscientiously on his official deeds. Strict attention to public relations was an important factor in his wide personal popularity. In addition to periodic press conferences, monthly meetings of the Governor's Council were a forum for announcements on administration affairs. Monthly "Report to the People" radio broadcasts were an effective device, not only for prodding the legislature but for rendering a factual accounting to the voters. His gubernatorial campaigns and citizen conferences were also occasions for such publicity.

Warren's belief in cooperative endeavor between citizens and government was closely related to his appeal for unity among different interests in California. He appeared before numerous organizations and gatherings to emphasize it. He remarked to the Commonwealth Club in San Francisco: "As in all difficult and

---

[3] Earl Warren, "Building for the Future in the West," *State Government*, XIX, No. 1 (Jan., 1946), 4.

[4] Address to California Real Estate Association, Oct. 7, 1943, *Warren Speeches* (in State Library, Sacramento).

complex undertakings in life, our postwar problems must be
approached with a unity of purpose . . . We can't advance by
cultivating hatreds, prejudices, or engaging in needless controversy. Progress is never made by looking for things to oppose.
It is made by looking for things to support."[5] Warren commented
in this vein to the legislature in 1947: "Solving these problems
in the interests of a state of over nine million people is our joint
responsibility. We can make a partnership of our task if we will
. . . In such a partnership, we should be able to find areas of
agreement that will make your deliberations fruitful for the entire
state . . . It means we must recognize that a thorough consideration of human problems transcends partisanship. It obligates us
to cooperate for the common good without regard to party,
faction, or personality. . . ."[6]

The Governor welcomed thoughts from interest groups, and
those of nearly every complexion found him respectful of their
convictions. He usually sounded out the ones most concerned
when devising his legislative platforms. Yet he always reserved
final judgment for himself, consistent with his personal interpretation of the public welfare. In a sense he felt obliged to represent
simultaneously the corporations, small businessmen, workers,
professional people, farmers, pensioners, and unorganized
citizenry of California. His periodic citizen conferences brought
together group representatives from many walks of life in a joint
enterprise for resolving state issues.

Warren therefore came into contact with a diversity of interests in his efforts to stimulate unity among them and to acquire
data necessary to develop public programs. His pragmatic mentality and desire for the facts involved a gradual digestion of
varying opinion. He usually abstained from promoting any
measure until all its ramifications had been investigated. This
often made him look more a follower than a leader in offering
legislation. Some of his ideas, such as state health insurance and

---

[5] Address, Jan. 7, 1944, *Warren Speeches.*
[6] *Inaugural Address of January 6, 1947* (Sacramento: 1947), p. 1.

disability subsidies under unemployment insurance, had been advanced earlier. Warren profited from the fact that his predecessor, Democratic Governor Culbert Olson, had already sponsored items like health insurance, higher old age pensions, and improved protection for workingmen. This made subsequent approval of some of them easier, since they were not so radical when Warren became chief executive. Robert E. Burke claimed that Olson's most lasting contribution was that of an educator. He paved the way for reforms sought by his successor. He further states that a popular Sacramento story has it that conservatives considered that their chief difficulties with Earl Warren stemmed from the fact that Olson had departed without cleaning out the governor's desk.[7]

The purpose of cooperative action and unity was to resolve public questions more effectively. His practical bent gave Warren a preoccupation with problem solving. Perhaps his major objective was to ameliorate, by the most appropriate means, those everyday concerns facing the California populace. To quote him directly: "My policy has been—and is—one of deciding, first of all, which problems are most urgent; and second, how they can be resolved. I try to meet, evaluate and solve the problems as they arise. I try never to let my day-to-day decisions be colored by considerations of what those decisions may mean at the next general election."[8]

The Chief Executive had some personal appreciation of these problems. A man of middle-income status, with a large family of six children, Warren was exposed to the same economic anxieties as others in his class. Moreover, he was a career public servant with no intention of leaving governmental pursuits. One of his former associates reported that when Warren was Alameda district attorney he was offered the job of chief counsel for an Oakland banking firm. He declined because it would involve

---

[7] Robert E. Burke, *Olson's New Deal for California* (Berkeley: Univ. of California Press, 1953), p. 233.

[8] Oliver Carlson, "Warren of California," *American Mercury*, XLVI, No. 293 (May, 1948), 543.

working for a specific, private interest. His disposition was such that he could be satisfied only with a public post.[9]

His background and attitudes undoubtedly made Warren more pliant in using state machinery than most members of his party. Conservative Republican Assemblyman Harold Levering of Los Angeles maintained that Warren had already developed "progressive views" when he was elevated to the highest state office because he "had always lived off the public payroll."[10]

The Doctrine of Social Progress

Thus Warren believed in moderate but steady improvement for persons of modest means through state action. Eventually he described this view with the phrase *social progress.* A commentary on this theory was delivered by the Governor before alumni of the College of Medical Evangelists in 1949. The topic was compulsory health insurance, which he would continue to advocate despite its denunciation as socialistic by reactionary Republicans.

A distinction had to be made between socialism and social progress. The Chief Executive cited early-day condemnations of some of our fundamental institutions as socialism. Considerable ill will was once aroused over the notion of public schools, and attacks were launched on municipal ownership of water and power. Yet during the depression-ridden thirties businessmen failed to cry "collectivism" regarding government loans to troubled commercial ventures, bankers found nothing revolutionary in federal guarantee of bank deposits, and farmers favored national subsidies for self-protection. A social advance is labeled radical or reasonable depending upon "whose economic needs are at stake and whose ox is being gored."

Warren spoke of the original opposition of organized medicine to the Mayo Clinic and of the expulsion of doctors from the

---

[9] James Oakley, former judge of the Superior Court of Sacramento County, former executive secretary to Gov. Warren, former deputy to District Atty. Warren in Alameda County, and former deputy attorney general to Warren. Interview, Feb. 20, 1958.

[10] Interview, Feb. 14, 1957.

American Medical Association for participation in some early group-prepayment plans. Medical antagonism to his own health proposal was but another variant of such behavior—an objection to a state project devised to relieve human distress. He concluded: "We have a great obligation to demonstrate that our American system has the strength and resiliency to solve any of the problems of American life.

"It has been said truly that if we resist improvements because they involve changes, we will eventually get changes without improvements. . . .

"The hope of our future depends upon our ability to convince this group [the low-wage families of the nation] that our democratic processes can solve the problems of American life, including their own, better than any other system on earth."[11]

It might be inferred that Warren was a man who developed in office, that his viewpoint evolved from conservative to liberal only over the course of his administration.[12] Yet he seemingly held to the principle of social progress when he first became California's chief executive, although his convictions were not then widely recognized or expressed with that phrase. True, the first 1943 program was not as progressive in tenor as the programs of subsequent years. The new governor probably moved at a slower pace initially in order to assess the Sacramento political climate and to avoid provoking antipathy while building support for later years. Furthermore, wartime dictated concentration on matters of defense.

Still, the praise lavished by Democratic lawmakers upon several 1945 Warren proposals gave him a liberal reputation at this early date in his gubernatorial career. Assembly minority leader Alfred Robertson of Santa Barbara said the Governor had adopted several dogmas of the Roosevelt administration. "He's joined the Democratic party," Robertson held.[13] Assemblyman

---

[11] *Sacramento Bee,* Oct. 8, 1949, p. 40.

[12] See Herbert L. Phillips, "Warren of California," *Nation,* 174, No. 21 (May 24, 1952), 495-97. Phillips does not claim this but employs the phrase in discussing the theory in his article.

[13] *Sacramento Bee,* Jan. 9, 1945, p. 1.

Julian Beck of Los Angeles, Robertson's successor, felt that Warren's pronouncements that year "put the Democratic party on the spot and almost deprived it of a separate program."[14] "He's trying to out-New Deal the New Deal!" exclaimed Democratic Assemblyman George Collins of San Francisco.[15]

In varying degrees most men are tempered in outlook by the sobering effects of office holding, and Warren was no exception. However, a better explanation in his case than the "development-in-office" theory would seem appropriate. Based upon his personal character and maturation through a lengthy public career, it is plausible to assume that the doctrine of social progress was fairly well implanted in his mind before he entered the executive mansion. Former Governor Olson indicated there was some confusion in the minds of many people as to where Warren stood politically. Having been generally classified as a traditional Republican before his promotion to the top state post, Warren appeared to take on a more liberal bearing after becoming governor. A number of people rationalized that his convictions had seemingly shifted only because they had erred in their initial assessment of them. However, those positions which Warren had occupied earlier dealt mainly with matters of law enforcement and granted him little opportunity to voice a political creed. When he entered the statehouse he came into an office where his views were given full vent for the first time.[16] Bernard Brennan stated the gist of it in somewhat exaggerated fashion: "Earl Warren of 1943 is the same person in beliefs as Earl Warren, Chief Justice of the United States."[17]

---

[14] Mr. Beck is now a judge of the Superior Court of Los Angeles County, was a judge of the Municipal Court of Los Angeles, and served for a time as legislative secretary to Gov. Edmund G. Brown. Interview, May 11, 1956.

[15] *Sacramento Bee,* Jan. 9, 1945, p. 1.

[16] Mr. Olson, now deceased, served as California governor from 1939 to 1943, being defeated by Warren in 1942. Interview, Jan. 3, 1958.

[17] Interview, Dec. 27, 1956. Former Judge Frederick F. Houser of the Los Angeles County Superior Court, and lieutenant governor of California under Warren's first term, from 1943 to 1947, disagrees with this argument. He felt that Warren's viewpoint was quite conservative until his elevation

By embracing ideas resembling those held by many Democrats, Warren helped to categorize himself as a progressive Republican, and his progressivism strengthened his nonpartisan reputation. Recommendations of a liberal nature inevitably stamped the Governor as somewhat nonpartisan in that they failed to enjoy the undivided backing of GOP functionaries and legislators. In turn, this reinforced his own wish for relaxation in party connections and caused some Republicans to take an even cooler attitude toward him. Completing the circle, his lack of enthusiastic partisanship made him and his thoughts all the more acceptable to Democratic legislators and voters. Thus his progressivism and nonpartisanship were interwined and mutually supportive. And Warren's political independence was certainly manifest in his campaigns for the California governorship.

---

to the governorship. His past record indicated this. He was boosted politically in Alameda County and thereafter primarily by the Knowland family and their *Oakland Tribune*. His more "liberal" stance after 1943 was basically an appearance, stimulated by political expediency and not by fundamental belief. Interview, Apr. 15, 1959.

Politics, Warren Style: Campaigns, Program Development, and Legislative Relations

PART TWO

Politics, Warren Style: Campaigns,
Program Development,
and Legislative Relations

CHAPTER II

Earl Warren: The Political Campaigner

Earl Warren's three races for California governor, in 1942, 1946, and 1950, provide considerable evidence of his independent political approach. He was a registered Republican who performed official and voluntary chores for his party, yet he was the epitome of individualism in office seeking. Nearly all phases of his gubernatorial battles had an aura of self-sufficiency. He consistently refused to campaign with fellow Republicans on the same ballot. Indeed, he resisted mightily and successfully attempts to lure him into endorsing them. He criticized his second- and third-term opponents for trying to tie all GOP aspirants into a convenient "package" to be disposed of by an aroused Democratic voting majority united behind its own party slate. In short, Warren wanted to avoid identification in the public eye as a "typical" Republican while campaigning.

Warren's electioneering organizations were strictly his own entities. While Republicans held most of the important positions in them, they were picked solely because of personal qualifications and contacts with the candidate, and not partisan affiliation. This was contrary to the relatively closed and hierarchical arrangements in many parts of the country. Democrats were welcome and were frequently brought into the Warren fold with high rank and responsibility. The names of many other Democrats were used for purposes of publicity. The financing of Warren's vote-searching endeavors was an additional study in shunning partisan shackles. Virtually a total separation was practiced from the dollar-raising ventures of other GOP hopefuls and the party generally. Warren also eschewed party matters while stumping the state. His individual record and views on

state questions were the only relevant points at issue so far a
he was concerned.

There were sound reasons for this course. Electoral succes
comes easiest to a candidate who plays down obvious or poten
tial weaknesses and stresses matters most likely to strengthen hi
popular rating. It would not prove advantageous at the polls to
stand like Gibraltar on principles of rock-ribbed Republicanism
in a constituency with a Democratic bulge on the electoral rolls
But an independent stance by a nominal Republican in such a
state, long shy on disciplined voting, could pay handsomely in
ballots. Warren was realist and opportunist enough to play it
that way and to do it successfully.

The word *opportunist* brings to mind anything but visions
of nobility, and Warren's strategy and tactics did not endear him
to those who worshiped at the altar of firmly held conviction.
Still, his version of the game was more in keeping with the spirit
of American public life. The foremost goal of a campaigner or of
a party is to capture the machinery of government. Only the
victorious can see a sizable portion of their program (even if
often in a compromised form) made into public policy. Abiding
by unyielding principle when the political atmosphere is un-
congenial will usually result in defeat; consequently desired
proposals will not see the legal light of day. So perhaps it is
adherence to "principle" in politics to face up to the "givens" of
the clime and time, act to secure the desired office, and then toil
diligently for the chosen goals from the vantage point of public
power. Warren astutely dedicated himself to that end. Pragmatic?
—to be sure. Unprincipled?—doubtful. Purposeful—most certainly. In short, the sacrifice of partisan loyalty was the price
Warren paid for action and accomplishment.

Campaign Organization

A spirit of autonomy was quite manifest in Earl Warren's
campaign organization. He laid down few firm rules for those in
charge. One rule that he did consistently invoke bordered on a

catechism: there was to be absolutely no fusion with the electioneering efforts of other Republicans or with any that might be
conducted by the ordinarily moribund party central committees.
Thomas J. Cunningham wrote: ". . .'multiple service' among campaign workers was discouraged completely. . . . While in their
[other GOP contenders'] headquarters they might be carrying
Warren literature, that was not true to any observable extent in
the Warren headquarters. There were people coming in . . . who
were voting a Democratic ticket other than Earl Warren, and to
have had Republican literature around would have divorced them
from our campaign."[1]

Initial preparations for each of Warren's three successful runs
for the statehouse were made informally. He discussed the broad
outlines of a campaign framework with a few friends in different
parts of California several months before the primaries. These
were mostly Republicans to begin with, but those of Democratic
persuasion were included as developments proceeded. A telephone call from the Governor early in 1950 to Victor Hansen of
Los Angeles resulted in a casual meeting of the two men at the
Jonathan Club. Hansen agreed to supervise the undertaking that
year in the Southland and was asked to build a structure along
the general lines discussed. Warren allowed his lieutenants as
much discretion as possible, permitting them to make their own
decisions on matters of organization, the appointment of subordinates, finance, and strategy. He tried to create the impression
that his entourage was composed of people from both parties
interested personally in Earl Warren's good fortune at the polls,
and sufficiently interested to work for that end largely on their
own.

Sectional committees, such as the one Hansen headed, constituted the mainstays of Warren's campaigns. There was one for
the northern and another for the southern half of California, a

---

[1] Thomas J. Cunningham (R), vice president and general counsel of
the University of California, former judge of the Superior Court of Los
Angeles County, former member of the California State Assembly, and
1946 campaign chairman for Warren in Southern California. Letter to me
Apr. 29, 1959.

pattern long conventional in statewide electoral pursuits. Each unit had freedom in guiding the vote drive and in soliciting and spending money in its area. Some liaison was afforded through contact with Warren and a few of his aides. The exact lines of the setup within each major region varied from one election to the next, although the general contours were easily discerned. Each sectional committee was under a chairman, the ranking officer accountable for overseeing the campaign in his part of the state. Presiding in each locality over Warren's three governorship contests were the following men, all Republicans, surrounded by a bevy of assistants from both major parties: *North*—Irving Martin, publisher of the *Stockton Record* (1942); Murray Draper, San Francisco lawyer (1946); Thomas J. Mellon, San Francisco business leader and financier (1950); *South*—Raymond Haight, Los Angeles lawyer and 1934 gubernatorial candidate on the Progressive and Commonwealth tickets (1942); Thomas J. Cunningham, then a Los Angeles lawyer and now vice president and general counsel, University of California (1946); Victor R. Hansen, Los Angeles lawyer, former judge of the county superior court there and former director of the Antitrust Division of the federal Justice Department under Dwight Eisenhower (1950). These men picked their principal helpers. Usually included were at least two vice chairmen and two field men, an executive body, a finance committee, a speakers'-bureau chief, a publicity director, a manager, and a "contacts division" leader. County leaders were also crucial to each enterprise.

Surveillance and coordination of the campaign within a group of counties or large districts were the prime responsibilities of the vice chairmen. Hansen in 1950 named assistant Louis Burke to supervise the vote hunt in the Southland outside Los Angeles and assigned assistant William D. Campbell to guide the effort in the city. Field men inaugurated county and lesser units and served as communications links between those localities and the main office. Maynard Givens worked under Hansen in 1950 as organizer of and contact man with Warren committees in the seven Southern California counties of Imperial, Orange, Riverside, Santa Barbara, San Bernardino, San Diego, and Ventura.

The same task was performed that year by his colleague Lionel Campbell within big Los Angeles County; there he established and synchronized units which generally followed incorporated cities within that jurisdiction.

Each county was customarily administered by a single authority, although occasionally two or more smaller ones were joined under one person. Co-chairmen were sometimes selected to placate various interests, to put down jealousies or, more frequently, to cast a bipartisan net over the operation. City or district structures of differing sizes and shapes were fashioned in larger counties. In 1950 San Francisco had six subdivisions, carved out for the locales of Bay View, Haight-Ashbury, Marina, Sunset, West Portola, and North Beach. An executive directorate of some ten persons was formed by the sectional chairman for general advice in meeting the problems of electioneering.

The important finance committee embraced as many persons of affluence or with connections in the world of high finance as volunteered or could be drafted. Usually numbering about fifteen men and women, this body was entrusted with raising the requisite cash. The dollars collected were then dispensed for objectives specified by the chairman, who was technically accountable for all money taken in and spent by the organization. Preston Hotchkiss, Southern California finance chairman in 1950, attested to the opulence of some who served with devotion and open purse on these fund-raising entities. His dossier reads as follows: the president of Founders' Fire and Marine Insurance; a principal stockholder and director of Blue Diamond Corporation, of California Trust, of Pacific Mutual Life Insurance, of Pacific Telephone and Telegraph, of Grand Central Garage, and of Yosemite Park and Curry Company. The chief of the speakers' bureau was charged with lining up those from both major parties eager to ride the "chicken and mashed potato" circuit as spokesmen for Warren. He also arranged dates and details for their appearances.

All of the functionaries above were unpaid individuals who volunteered to push Warren for California governor. The same was true of members of the respective committees, whose "assignments" often consisted of nothing more than being listed in pamphlets and newspaper ads. Some of them opened up their pocketbooks; others put in time on the telephone or in mailing letters and circulars. Both officers and committee members were, in the main, citizens prominent in their professions or communities. They were chosen principally for the prestige they could lend to the operation, and not for their expertise in conducting campaigns. For expertise, reliance was heaviest on two salaried officers, who were most involved in daily routine.

One of these was the publicity director. He commanded a retinue of writers, press agents, communications experts, advertising advisers, and clerical assistants. Head publicist for the Southland in 1950 was Niver Beman, who controlled a staff that composed stories for various journals, a news-clipping service that furnished releases for smaller papers, a subordinate who prepared material for distribution to Democratic groups, and a representative who arranged radio and television shows for Warren. Beman and his aides decided on the details and disposition of printing in consultation with commercial firms, although basic advertising format was cleared with Warren and the area leaders. Warren had entrusted not only publicity but overall statewide direction of his 1942 race to the Whitaker and Baxter public relations firm. Reacting against their insistence on almost complete domination in that contest and infuriated over the partnership's "sabotage" of his compulsory health insurance proposals on behalf of the California Medical Association, the Governor dropped the husband-wife team after his first win. He put his faith in a more decentralized system thereafter. However, in all three statehouse campaigns each sectional aggregation depended on a manager for detailed administration; a part of his task was to work with the chairman of the contacts division to set up auxiliary committees.

These last-named "nonparty" bodies have long been features of California politics and are increasingly found in other states and nationally. They are designed in particular to attract prominent persons not disposed to associate themselves with more partisan operations and to create an impression of broad backing for a candidate in specific sectors of society. Frequently composed of enthusiastic personal backers of some worth, they can also constitute a ready reserve of financial donors, doorbell ringers, literature dispensers, and general arm twisters on behalf of their heroes. Illustrative in recent presidential contests were the Citizens for Eisenhower-Nixon, Volunteers for Stevenson, Citizens for Kennedy-Johnson, Citizens for Nixon-Lodge, and Citizens for Goldwater-Miller. Many units of this type, whether national or state, scarcely function in practice and exist largely on paper.

In the Warren campaigns these bodies were labeled "divisions" of the area headquarters, although rarely did they participate in overt electioneering. Their principal purpose was simply to dramatize support for Warren from assorted components of California's citizenry. Occasionally they held meetings to listen to the candidate himself or to other speakers. Some of their more energetic members made telephone calls or delivered talks for Warren. Most of them contributed money.

Auxiliary committees were established in various areas in all three of Warren's gubernatorial battles. They were formed for war veterans, women, business and professional people, labor representatives, members of minority races, public officials, sports figures, Democrats, and a host of others. A 1942 gathering of some two hundred physicians and surgeons conveyed an impression of widespread medical affection for Warren in San Francisco, something that might have pleased him more in subsequent elections after his imbroglio with California's doctors over health insurance. Sitting on its executive committee, ironically, was Dr. Alison R. Kilgore, who later became president of the C.M.A. and a key assailant of Warren's government health plan. The Republican standard-bearer's Southern California aides constructed a Loyal Democrats for Warren group in 1942 under movie actor Leo Carillo. The year 1946 saw Negroes for Warren come to life in the Southland, led by former U.C.L.A. football star Kenny Washington.

Clusters of laborers and veterans for Warren appeared in all three gubernatorial elections. A 1950 Northern California Labor Committee to promote the Chief Executive was chaired by Milton

Table 1

SOME DEMOCRATIC PARTICIPANTS
IN 1950 WARREN CAMPAIGN

Name	Campaign Position, Location
George C. Cloney	Co-chairman, Humboldt County
Phillip R. Collins	Vice chairman, Yolo County
J. Thomas Crowe	Vice chairman, Tulare County
J. H. Davies	Chairman, City of Long Beach
Clifford Driskell	Chairman, Kings County
Paul Elmore	Co-chairman, Lake County
Philip J. Fay	Vice chairman, San Francisco County
Patrick J. Freeman	Co-chairman, Santa Cruz County
Lester M. Ireland	Vice chairman, Yolo County
Ray Jackson	Chairman, Placer County
Fred W. McKechnie	Vice chairman, Northern California
A. A. McKinnon	Chairman, El Dorado County
Frank S. Oliver	Co-chairman, Santa Cruz County
Jack E. O'Neill	Chairman, Fresno County
Alvin Pecchenino	Co-chairman, Calaveras County
Odillo Restano	Co-chairman, Tuolumne County
Albert J. Ruffo	Chairman, Santa Clara County
Ralph W. Rutledge	Co-chairman, Colusa County
George B. Sausmon	Co-chairman, Amador County
Marion M. Snodgrass	Co-chairman, Contra Costa County
Ernest A. Vernon	Co-chairman, Alameda County
Charles Wakefield	Co-chairman, Kern County

Source: *Los Angeles Times*, Apr. 30, 1950, p. 19; *Sacramento Bee*, Apr. 7, 1950, p. 8; *San Francisco Chronicle*, Mar. 31, 1950, p. 7; Apr. 26, 1950, p. 8.

Maxwell, international vice president of the Amalgamated Meat Cutters and Butcher Workmen of America. A veterans' Warren for Governor unit in the Southland that year was supervised by Norman M. "Pat" Lyon, founder and commander of American Legion Aviation Post 350 in Los Angeles and a man with a sizable list of credits in county, state, and national Legion affairs. Helping Lyon as vice chairmen were Louis Van Iansel and Leon V. "Mickey" McCardle, both medal recipients in World War II. A unique San Francisco group in 1950 was the Warren for Governor Nationality Committee. It was made up of representatives from seventeen different ethnic groups, divided almost evenly between Republicans and Democrats.

An outstanding feature of Warren's drives for the California governorship was his use of Democrats, encompassing those from the rank and file as well as a sprinkling of party functionaries and public officials. Often "members" of sectional and county bodies, they sometimes were made vice chairmen, chairmen or managers. Exemplary were such men as Fred W. McKechnie, 1950, second-in-command in Northern California, who was put in charge of the Sacramento Valley region, and Phillip J. Fay, vice chairman for San Francisco that year. The range of Democratic participation in Warren's campaign structure by 1950 is evident from an examination of Table 1.

Many Warren auxiliary committees had a generous contingent of Democrats. Indeed, bodies constituted entirely of people with that partisan designation were inaugurated each time. Illustrative of this bipartisan image building were two 1950 organizations, one for Northern and another for Southern California. The former was under San Francisco contractor Robert McCarthy, father of Republican John McCarthy, Marin County state senator and former Senate minority leader. It even had a few public-office holders and party committeemen on its roster. Recorded were such Democratic luminaries as Fresno State Senator Hugh Burns, now president pro tempore of the Senate; State Senator Luther Gibson of Vallejo; Belle Colledge, former Sacramento mayor; Patrick McDonough, past chairman of the Alameda County Central Committee; and Clem Butler, formerly on the Sonoma County Central Committee. This recruitment of men and women affiliated with the opposition camp again underscored Warren's desire for political separateness. It certainly pointed up his realization of the need to enlist backing from the party with a strong majority of the electorate if he was to triumph at the polls.

Warren stressed to both Democrats and Republicans who joined him in the campaigns that he assumed they did so only out of agreement with his past achievements and governmental philosophy. Their participation was not to be looked upon as a claim for future favor. He put it in these words in announcing himself as a candidate, for the last time: "I have never tried to maintain a political machine, and I have none at the present time. I will start from scratch immediately to build up a campaign organization that will help me to present my candidacy to the people. There will be room for anyone who desires to help. . . . When the campaign is over, I will disband it, and if re-elected, will continue to run the office independently, surrounding myself with the best people available to me, regardless of politics."[2]

Campaign Finance

Legal restrictions on raising and spending money for political purposes abound throughout the United States. These taboos, prevalent at both national and state levels, have combined with the decentralized character of American political parties and traditions of localism in politics to place on the shoulders of the individual candidate the prime responsibility for covering the costs he incurs while electioneering. Years of pronounced paralysis in much of California's party apparatus and a deeply ingrained tradition of separate vote-seeking have meant that aspirants for public office there are thrown back on their own resources even more than elsewhere, a situation quite prevalent when Warren was state chief executive. The gathering and dispensation of funds on Warren's behalf were done almost solely by his own committees, quite apart from the fiscal operations of other Republicans. Warren declined to implicate himself in the details of campaign finance, leaving them to his associates. Yet he was never loath to emphasize that donations would be welcomed from all Californians, regardless of their party. He strove not only for partisan autonomy but also freedom from obligation

---

[2] Opening Campaign Address, Feb. 3, 1950, *Warren Speeches*.

to pursuers of special privilege. In his first try for the state's highest office, in 1942, he was the beneficiary of heavy largesse from several oil companies; nevertheless, the Governor later called for greatly enlarged taxes on gasoline and oil products to underwrite California's vast highway development program beginning in 1947, much to the mortification of many industry leaders. They felt the Chief Executive to be something of an ingrate.

There are many loopholes in the reporting of campaign contributions and expenditures, both federal and state. The general notion behind the regulating laws is to publicize and to limit the size and nature of receipts and disbursements. But these objectives are but imperfectly attained and California's statute definitely contains its share of shortcomings. Indeed, the documents filed by candidates and their committees are very superficial and incomplete. Candidates must render personal accounts for the June primary as well as the November runoff, a requirement found neither in the federal provisions nor in those of many other states. During the Warren years, committees formed on behalf of a contender had to file statements for the final contest only. That stipulation has since been amended to apply to the June balloting also. Yet many of these bodies fail to comply on either occasion because of a dearth of adequate penalties and enforcement, a fairly standard curse across the country. California and several other states compel the various aspirants and their electioneering organizations to bare their fiscal secrets only *after* the ballots are counted. This drawback can allow for the doctoring of transcripts to conform to legalities; and the rules are quite permissive in the first instance.

California shares with the national government and many state governments another flaw in its corrupt-practices laws; they are largely deprived of comprehensive, meaningful, and understandable data in the final declarations of both committees and individuals. In California most of these monuments to evasion bear the telling title "*Summary* Statement of Campaign Contributions and Expenditures" (italics mine). Office seekers put down only those sums known to them alone. Warren made this assertion in 1950: "Committees in aid of my campaign were formed in Southern California and in Northern California and also in many counties and cities in the state. These committees independently undertook to raise funds for their activities in aid of my election. This report, however, includes only the contributions and expenditures which are within my knowledge."[3] Here was a confession that mirrored another deficiency which still persists in California's code and in that of many other jurisdictions, a lack of responsibility concentrated on the candidate himself. Indeed, the use of the word *summary* in California is misleading. There is no summation that totals all cash transactions for each candidate, the committees, and whatever party units may have participated.

Thus these financial documents cannot be taken as accurate compilations of all assets taken in and paid out during a campaign. Yet in Warren's case they do convey some idea of his independent political demeanor. All statements filed by him and his committees in each gubernatorial race, with the amounts collected and disbursed, are given in Table 2. Warren made his own reports for all three contests, although the figures he presented were well below those tallied by his sectional units.

Most of the resources publicized for his 1942 runoff were filtered through a "finance committee" that was undoubtedly the Southern California treasury. Every dollar taken in by the main Southland organization, which also drew up its own declaration, passed through that body. There was no separate recording for a northern group that year. The Loyal Democrats for Warren did deposit a written affadavit in Sacramento, the sole item submitted by an auxiliary association. Warren won both principal primaries in 1946 and faced no two-man race in November, so no committee tabulations were made that year. The only acknowl-

---

[3] Campaign Statement for the General Election of 1950, Nov. 21, 1950. The information that follows in this section was taken from the campaign financial statements filed by Warren personally, by committees working on his behalf, and by Republican party groups, in all three gubernatorial contests, of 1942, 1946, and 1950. They are located in the archives of the office of the secretary of state, Sacramento.

CONTRIBUTIONS AND EXPENDITURES FOR WARREN GUBERNATORIAL CAMPAIGNS

Year	Personal Report		Committee Reports		
	Contributions	Expenditures	Committee	Total Contributions	Total Expenditures
1942					
Primary	$ 2,715.00	$ 2,631.48	Loyal Democrats Warren-for-Governor Committee	$ 23,827.36	$ 23,827.36
General	1,996.00	1,996.00	Warren-for-Governor Finance Committee	121,013.00	124,877.59
1946					
Primary	11,766.16	11,788.16			
General					
1950					
Primary	$29,268.00	$28,757.47	Northern California Warren-for-Governor Finance Committee	$145,770.33	$145,770.33
General	41,573.00	41,281.69	Warren-for-Governor Finance Committee of Southern California	119,734.75	119,734.75
			Warren-for-Governor Committee for Santa Barbara	980.00	978.45
			Warren-for-Governor Headquarters, San Bernardino	1,761.56	2,929.83
			Warren Campaign Committee of Sacramento County	17,328.03	17,328.03
			Warren-for-Governor Committee, Kern County	7,375.00	8,723.36

Source: Files of the office of secretary of state, Sacramento.

edgment that any money had changed hands then was an announcement of a rather paltry sum by the Governor himself. The 1950 third-term duel marked the greatest display of candor by his supporters. That years units from both ends of the state and in four counties took note of their fiscal doings.

Warren made scant use of the party apparatus in paying for his electioneering ventures, although available evidence on this point is far too limited for elaboration relative to the 1942 and 1946 contests. However, it became more obvious in his third try for the statehouse, following the 1949 creation of the United Republican Finance machinery. In 1950 the Governor received only a small proportion of all allotments from GOP groups. What help he got from them was pallid when compared with that given to other Republican nominees.

Table 3 provides more evidence of Warren's individualistic political style. The $878.50 tendered him by the Los Angeles United Republican Finance Committee in 1950 was little enough by itself. It appears infinitesimal when contrasted with the $35,862.17 furnished the one other statewide Republican standard-bearer named in that report, attorney-general candidate Edward S. Shattuck, and it hardly stands comparison with the $119,734.75 accounted for by Warren's own Southland organization (Table 2). The $7,375.00 collected by the Governor's Kern County friends that year stands in bold relief alongside the token tribute of $100.00 sent to him by that county's official party. In Long Beach several hundred dollars were spent in 1950 on ministering to the needs of Republicans Richard Nixon for United State senator, Craig Hosmer for congressman, Herbert Klocksiem for assemblyman, and Edward S. Shattuck for attorney general. Not a cent found its way into Warren's coffers. Indeed, the relatively meager sums conferred on the Chief Executive by each partisan organization appearing in Table 3 are the more striking when it is remembered that the gubernatorial battle ordinarily demands the heaviest outlay. Payments to Warren were not only the lowest in all documents turned in by GOP groups in 1950, they were even below those given to nominees for local office.

CAMPAIGN CONTRIBUTIONS BY CALIFORNIA REPUBLICAN BODIES, 1950

Organization	Amounts and Objects of Contributions	
United Republican Finance Committee of California, Los Angeles division	*Total Received*	$422,749.49
	Expenditures for Candidates:	
	Patrick J. Hillings, Congress	$ 1,050.00
	Edward S. Shattuck, Attorney General	35,862.17
	Earl Warren, Governor	878.50
Kern County Republican Central Committee	*Total Received*	20,698.00
	Expenditures for Candidates:	
	Pat Kelly, Assembly	2,750.00
	Richard M. Nixon, U.S. Senate	2,200.00
	Earl Warren, Governor	100.00
	Thomas H. Werdel, Congress	3,000.00
United Republican Finance Committee of Long Beach	*Total Received*	$ 7,321.50
	Expenditures for Candidates:	
	Craig Hosmer, Congress	$ 1,487.50
	Herbert Klocksiem, Assembly	717.55
	Richard M. Nixon, U.S. Senate	838.25
	Edward S. Shattuck, Attorney General	300.00
	Earl Warren, Governor	0.00
Republican Central Committee of Stanislaus County	*Total Received*	Not Listed
	Expenditures for Candidates:	
	Oakley Hunter, Congress	3,154.53
	Richard M. Nixon, U.S. Senate	1,264.53
	Edward S. Shattuck, Attorney General	898.19
	Earl Warren, Governor	637.36

Source: Files of the office of secretary of state, Sacramento.

Campaign Style: Political Independence
and Personal Government

In America, election campaigns for high public office, whether national or state, are executed in accord with a broad strategy that fixes their general tone and the major themes to be stressed. Eisenhower's re-election fight in 1956 was pitched on a high plane of morality and sincerity; stable leadership was the prime Johnson message against Goldwater in 1964. The November outcome is also conditioned by an image of the aspirant implanted in voters' minds, in turn contingent upon the over-all battle plan and the larger setting that shapes any campaign. In 1932 Roosevelt was dramatized as a "daring, resolute champion of action" against a "timid, hesitant, irresolute" Hoover.[4]

Earl Warren adhered to a fundamental strategy and tried to portray himself in a basic way to California's electorate when running for governor in 1942, 1946, and 1950. He emphasized political independence and personal accountability. He was by no means unique in that respect, for many White House, senatorial, and gubernatorial nominees have taken a nonpartisan tack either by necessity or by preference. For one whose party trails badly in the registration statistics, bipartisan overtures are dictated by cold arithmetic. Witness the stance taken by Richard Nixon in 1960, Senator Jacob Javits of New York in 1962, Michigan's Governor George Romney in 1964, or John Lindsay in his 1965 campaign for mayor of New York City.

Warren faced an even more compelling situation in California. An individualistic posture was essential for a Republican candidate seeking a statewide post at that time, given the Democratic preponderance in affiliated voters and the customs of political autonomy. Add to these facts of state public life a personal inclination toward independence and the die was cast for electioneering, Warren style. Warren first proclaimed his

---

[4] Raymond Moley, *After Seven Years* (New York: Harper, 1939), p. 26.

governorship ambitions in 1942 in these words: "I am a Republican, but . . . I shall seek the support of both parties. I can do this honorably because I am an independent, and therefore in a position to serve the people fairly, regardless of their politics or mine."[5]

Rarely absent from Warren's 1942 campaign appearances was his main theme, condensed into the slogan "leadership, not politics." He constantly reiterated one overriding goal: to reduce partisanship to a minimum in state government. There was a special reason for that tack then, regardless of his personal creed and the basic nature of California politics. For in a sense here was an instance of the office seeking the man. The country was at war and a mood of unity prevailed. Warren's earlier career as a nonpartisan law-enforcement officer and his cry to lessen partisanship in managing public business meshed well with the times. President Roosevelt himself had asked for a respite from narrow party politics for the duration, a fact Warren was never slow in citing to rank-and-file Democrats. Whenever his opponent, incumbent Governor Olson, implored the overwhelmingly Democratic electorate to reject the Attorney General's bid for political promotion because he was a registered Republican, Warren countered that such an attack only affirmed Olson's inability to adjust to the more conciliatory posture demanded by the existing crisis.

Warren constantly assailed the patent political bias of Culbert Olson. This he did before all types of audiences, even those purely GOP in makeup. To a conclave of Young Republicans he pressed for "an end to petty party politics which has hamstrung our state government in meeting its war obligations and which has let vital, critical jobs go undone. . . ."[6] He denounced the continual wrangling between governor and legislature. It was not a party feud but a quarrel that pitted one vindictive individual against the lawmakers in general. Warren went before

---

[5] Marjorie Dent Candee, ed., *Current Biography*, Fifteenth Annual Accumulation, 1954 (New York: H. W. Wilson, 1954), p. 636.

[6] Robert E. Burke, *Olson's New Deal for California* (Berkeley: Univ. of California Press, 1953), pp. 212-13.

no less a partisan assemblage than the state GOP convention to charge that this was "not a contest between the Republican and Democratic parties, for Governor Olson, by his arrogance, his blundering and his selfish manipulation . . . during a period of gravest emergency, has jeopardized the safety and welfare of the people of California."[7]

Olson employed the opposite strategy by continuously invoking partisan loyalty and tried persistently to associate himself with President Roosevelt: "The great majority of the voters of California are Democrats because they know our Democratic party is the party of the people and that the Republican party is the party of predatory interests, opposed to social gains and progressive economic policies. Our state and national administrations have proved their fidelity to the people's trust, and we Democrats go before the people squarely on our record of faithful performance."[8]

The Chief Executive lashed out severely at Warren's nonpartisan stand as primary time drew near. He reminded Democrats of "the ever-present fundamental issues upon which we *challenge* Republican party opponents who are hypocritically seeking Democratic votes . . . in Democratic primaries." The Governor condemned the GOP as "an aristocracy of wealth" and implored the brethren to "vote only for Democrats and not for any Republican whose name you may find on your ballot."[9] On the eve of the nomination he ripped into his antagonist: "Anyone who is so cowardly as to put on the cloak of nonpartisanship in an election like this, either acknowledges that he is a political eunuch and does not know what it is all about, or that he is a political hypocrite. This nonpartisan, non-political propaganda is a piece of colossal deceit. It is essentially a lie."[10] Whether insincere or not, Warren was obviously no novice. He won the Republican nod with ease over token opposition. (True to his staunch Democratic convictions, the Governor had declined to

---

[7] *Ibid.*, p. 219.

[8] Radio address, July 30, 1942, as quoted in Burke, pp. 215-16.

[9] *Ibid.*, p. 216.

[10] *Ibid.*

cross-file.) Warren rolled up a huge total on the Democratic side, his 404,778 ballots being not far behind the 514,144 polled by Olson.

Warren disavowed party solidarity throughout 1942. Frederick F. Houser, Republican nominee for lieutenant governor, told me that he urged the "head of the ticket" to run as a team. The then attorney general allegedly agreed to this shortly after the primaries; however, he had a change of heart as they entered the final campaign in September. Houser speculated that the presence of Democrat Robert Kenny in the runoff for attorney general had something to do with the gubernatorial aspirant's reversal of form.[11] Kenny and Warren were close personal friends, although they were destined to do battle for the state's highest office in 1946. There might have been a misunderstanding between Houser and Warren, but a more plausible explanation is that Warren, on second thought, decided that consistency demanded maintenance of his individuality and that Houser could prove a definite handicap. Indeed, Houser barely made it in November.

Whatever his reasoning, Warren asked both Democarts and Republicans right up to election day to come to his aid. He summarized his position in a debate with his foe: ". . . I am fully conscious and deeply appreciative of the fact that the votes I received at the primary . . . came from both major parties in almost equal numbers. . . . I give you my sacred pledge today that as governor I will conduct a nonpartisan administration. . . . I am a registered Republican, and have held office in the Republican party. And I believe in the party system in normal times. But this is not a Democratic war nor a Republican war. It is an American war." He promised a tenure unfettered by "ownership or control" by any faction and pledged that "no group will get special favors." He predicted that out of such a policy would "come a new birth of mutual confidence—a lessening of strife and dissension."[12] The final election was a decisive

---

[11] Interview, Apr. 15, 1959.

[12] Opening Statement at San Francisco Forum, Oct. 11, 1942, *Warren Speeches.*

victory for Earl Warren: 1,275,287 Californians cast their votes for him, while 932,995 stayed with Olson, a winning margin of 342,292.

Many ardent members of the GOP undoubtedly entertained the thought that with a return to peace Governor Warren would take more note of his Republican heritage. They were to be disappointed, for he maintained his individualistic brand of politics during the whole of his residence in Sacramento. He certainly gave full vent to it in both the 1946 and the 1950 campaigns. Furthermore, his quest for popular unity in resolving public issues was accentuated anew in the postwar period.

Warren opened his try for a second term, in 1946, by retracing his official performance in attacking the problems that continually beset the state: "Their solution cannot be found in narrow partisanship any more than world problems can be solved through extreme nationalism. They can be solved only through independent, humane, forward-looking and financially sound government. I am prepared to offer for the future that kind of approach to government—exactly as I have done in the past. . . ." He professed distaste for "machine politics" and vowed that he had no aspiration to head "any group or organization that would dominate the political life of this state." He said, perhaps a bit too innocently, "No man should be permitted to be both governor and a political boss." Californians could rest assured "that whenever I leave the governor's chair, I will return it to the people unencumbered, and without any political strings around it."[13] That guarantee was largely fulfilled as he took leave for Washington, D.C. The subsequent internecine warfare in Republican circles and the party's later fate in state politics certainly give credence to it.

The 1946 fight was the easiest for Warren. Yet it placed in sharpest focus two of the more important and specific applications of his larger approach to politics. His foremost Democratic challenger then was his friend and sometime supporter Robert W. Kenny, his successor as attorney general. Kenny seemed

---

[13] Radio Address, Mar. 18, 1946, *Warren Speeches.*

intent on coming to grips with the substance of Warren's governorship when he first entered the fray. He charged that the administration was guilty of "muddling through," was utterly devoid of any "blueprint" for meeting reconversion problems, and rested on nothing more than "pure opportunism." The state deserved forceful guidance instead of having to tolerate a predicament in which it "limps along . . . by a series of makeshift maneuvers based on the political expediency of the moment."[14] Yet as the dialogue quickened the Attorney General made little criticism of Warren on tangible issues. He failed to make clear what differences, if any, separated him from the Governor on key policies—no mean trick for any Democrat running against Earl Warren.

Rollin McNitt told me that Kenny was a "halfhearted" candidate, reluctant to enter the race against Warren. He virtually had to be pushed into the contest. There was a feeling among many Democratic leaders that unless the strongest possible Democrat ran for governor, the party chances in the 1948 presidential election would be impaired. Aside from Senator Sheridan Downey, Kenny was the only Democratic statewide officeholder and he was presumed to be the stronger possibility of the two. "The party stalwarts had to be given something to fight for to keep them in shape for 1948," remarked McNitt.[15]

Kenny concentrated on two topics: legislative-executive relations and the so-called package deal. First, he claimed that public questions could be better resolved if the Governor would steer his proposals through the legislative halls in a more positive manner. The Democrat blamed Warren for losing some of his "liberal" measures because he had not flexed sufficient partisan muscle to impress the Republican majority in either assembly or senate. This was not meant to imply bad faith in the Chief Executive; it was simply that his program was personal and not partisan and thus was handicapped from the outset. "Individual

[14] *Sacramento Bee,* Mar. 9, 1946, p. 4.

[15] Rollin McNitt (D), Los Angeles lawyer, former chairman of the Los Angeles County Democratic Central Committee. Interview, Apr. 18, 1959.

careerism," objected Kenny, was not enough for effective government. The sharp-witted Attorney General quipped: "Governor Warren was born on the wrong side of the political tracks. He is a poor little rich boy who would like to get out and play with the Democratic urchins, but his elderly legislative chaperons won't let him."[16] Warren defended what he called "open dealing" with the lawmakers. Contrary to Kenny's allegations, the need was to cultivate a disposition to compromise between the two branches of government, an absolute prerequisite to any meaningful assault on civic issues. The Governor insisted that those statutory setbacks which he did suffer were "inevitable results of our American system of divided responsibility."[17]

The 1946 debate also centered on the Attorney General's "package deal." Kenny suggested that party responsibility was crucial to productive administration, and for electoral purposes this meant a common front by the whole "slate." A man of his word, he sought to attach his campaign securely to the campaigns of other Democrats. The gambit met with stony silence in general and even chilly reception in some quarters. This was particularly true in the case of Edmund G. Brown, San Francisco's district attorney and Democratic entry for the post Kenny was vacating. Undaunted, the Attorney General continued to urge victory for everyone on the ballot affiliated with his party.

Warren's retort exhibited a keen appreciation of California's political temper. He frowned on any notion of boss rule and rapped the package concept as alien to state customs: "I don't think the independent voters of California want it," he opined.[18] He was correct in that assessment, for the Democratic parcel was torn asunder in the primaries. Fragments of it went on to the November runoff, although it was headless, for Robert Kenny fell by the wayside in June. Earl Warren had astounded the nation by capturing both major party nominations, the only governor in California's history to have accomplished that feat. Interestingly, Warren had made two exceptions to the no-

---

16 *Sacramento Bee*, Apr. 12, 1946, p. 4.
17 Campaign Luncheon Address, Apr. 24, 1946, *Warren Speeches*.
18 *Ibid.*

endorsement rule he otherwise uniformly applied to other Republican office seekers: he openly backed United States Senator William F. Knowland, his own 1945 appointee, to take over for the deceased Hiram Johnson, and Goodwin J. Knight (his eventual successor as chief executive) for lieutenant governor. However, the Governor was moved to such benevolence only in late fall. It is questionable whether he would have been so charitable had he himself faced a final election contest of any consequence.

The idea of partisan solidarity in electioneering came up again four years later. James Roosevelt, the 1950 Democratic standard-bearer, apparently did not fully comprehend the message conveyed by the 1946 results. He resurrected the package deal, and his fellow Democrats on the ballot were anything but overjoyed. Predictably, the opposite occurred on the Republican side, where Warren once again ignored the rest of the GOP ticket. He even felt the idea of a joint effort to be contrary to the very principle of the direct primary, in which each aspirant was "the keeper of his own conscience" and should "run on his own reputation and record."[19]

The Governor's aloofness that year was a principal cause of the ultimately renowned and durable feud between himself and Richard Nixon, then contending for the United States Senate. Earl Mazo, principal chronicler of Nixon's career, tells how the would-be senator cleverly won an approving nod from Warren.[20] A Nixon devotee followed Congresswoman Helen Gahagan Douglas, his Democratic opponent, to press conferences and constantly badgered her about her feelings on Roosevelt. She resisted any linkage to Roosevelt's campaign until the Friday before the polling, when she finally confessed: "I hope and pray he will be the next governor, and he will be, if the Democrats vote the Democratic ticket." Warren, questioned about his reaction to Mrs. Douglas' burst of candor, responded: "I have no intention of being coy about this situation. As always, I have

---

[19] *Sacramento Bee*, Apr. 26, 1950, p. 4.

[20] Details of the Warren-Nixon squabble and Mazo's interpretation of it are in Mazo's *Richard Nixon: A Political and Personal Portrait* (New York: Harper-Avon, 1960), pp. 76-77, 84-85.

kept my campaign independent from other campaigns. . . . In view of her statement, however, I might ask her how she expects I will vote when I mark my ballot for United States senator Tuesday." Jubilation reigned among the Nixonites. The interpretation got back to a most unhappy chief executive that he had been lured by the politically astute Nixon people into blessing the Whittier congressman for higher office. Mazo hints that Warren's refusal to assist Nixon in his first congressional battle in 1946, when he had "indirectly aided Nixon's Democratic opponent," was the start of the trouble. It was exacerbated in 1950 by the Governor's separateness and the belief among Nixon champions that Warren actually wanted to see the young representative defeated.

The bickering between the two men intensified in the 1952 presidential contest. There were accusations by some Warrenites that Nixon, having been told that his chances were excellent of becoming Eisenhower's vice-presidential running mate, sold out favorite-son White House hopeful Earl Warren. Contrary to Mazo's implications that this was not the case, my interviews lend considerable credence to the sellout theory. As one irrefutable authority put it—emphatically off the cuff—"Mr. Nixon was busy as a little bee on the Warren campaign train from Denver to Chicago wooing away the Governor's delegates to the Eisenhower cause."

The 1950 Nixon episode pointed up the individualistic note struck by the Governor again that year in the gubernatorial race. He threw his hat into the ring, for the third and final time, with now typical and familiar prose: "I am, as you know, a Republican. But I shall make no appeal to blind partisanship, or follow any other divisive tactics. I will submit my candidacy to all the people, as I have in the past. What we need to preserve in this state is unity instead of factionalism; good will instead of prejudice; and cooperation rather than dissention. I will promote these things by recognizing my public responsibility to all our citizens."[21]

_____

21 Opening Campaign Address, Feb. 3, 1950, *Warren Speeches.*

Significantly, the Korean conflict after June, 1950, provided a background more congenial to such a plea, an atmosphere similar to that prevalent in 1942. The Governor depicted his adversary as a man bent on disrupting the harmony so critical in prosecuting the latest war effort. He complained that "during these days of world tension, Mr. Roosevelt would divide us—party by party, group by group." Once more capitalizing upon the comments of a Democrat in the White House, Warren summoned to his cause the words of Harry S. Truman: ". . . above all, be sure that the candidates you vote for are not the kind of people who will try to divide us over petty issues or weaken our international position for purely partisan reasons." He endorsed that comment wholeheartedly and lived by it daily, the Governor contended, and "it would be well for our state if Mr. Roosevelt did likewise."[22]

Warren gave extra weight to his nonpartisan strategy and image through a radio round-table discussion with two notable Democrats. He was joined by Kenneth D. Holland, president of the Beverly Hills Bar Association and a pillar in that city's Democratic Club for years, and Harold Caulfield, an eminent lawyer active in San Francisco Democratic affairs. Together they recapitulated the Republican Chief Executive's attainments during two terms in office and ultimately got around to castigating Roosevelt. The two Democrats decried their party nominee's lack of experience and censured him for "deceit, political trickery, and distortion." Both men put Earl Warren's know-how and record of "good government" above partisanship.[23]

The Governor expressed appreciation for the past assistance he had received from rank-and-file Democrats. As if trying to point up a lesson in politics for his competitor, he lectured: "To know that their vision is not clouded by the political smog surrounding Mr. Roosevelt and his personal campaign of vilification is heartening. To be reassured that his appeal to blind partisanship instead of dispassionate reasoning is being appraised

---

[22] Radio Round Table discussion, Oct. 20, 1950, *Warren Speeches.*
[23] *Ibid.*

for its own inadequacy is encouraging. Californians are not blind partisans. . . . They want to make progress day-to-day. And they know it can best be done through tolerance, understanding, and cooperation on the part of everyone. . . ."[24] Again it was Earl Warren, not his rival, who proved the better politician in the California of that era. He ran up a huge popular plurality in November, downing Roosevelt by over one million votes. Indeed, in all three governorship contests he won the affection of a legion of Democrats through his nonpartisan pitch. Attuned to the realities of state public life, he consistently and handily surmounted a gigantic Democratic lead on the electoral rolls.

Warren's technique of toning down partisan attachments by no means stopped at California's borders. Illustrative was his vice-presidential candidacy in 1948 on a Republican slate headed by Thomas E. Dewey. An apparent advantage held by the GOP team in the polls induced both of them to pursue a plan of offending no one. This resulted in overgeneralization in their oratory and growing mass doubts regarding where they stood on urgent public questions. The stratagem played perfectly into the hands of a hard-hitting, specific, and eventually victorious Harry Truman. Still, the course of action agreed upon pleased Warren no end. It may even have been a factor in his selection as running mate to the New Yorker.

California's governor told many of his 1948 audiences that it was sheer delusion to assume that all good flowed from one partisan side and all evil from the other. Most people were aware that "good Americans are to be found in both parties. They realize that there are progressives and conservatives in the ranks of both. They know that party affiliation does not change human instinct, or affect loyalty to country, or transcend the fond hope of Americans for their children. No party has a patent on progress, a copyright on governmental principles, or a proprietary interest in the advances made in former days."[25]

To Warren it was the condition of the two great political coalitions and their leadership of the moment that determined

<hr>

24 *Ibid.*
25 Campaign Address, Sept. 16, 1948, *Warren Speeches.*

which would be granted the mantle of government. The one that inspired the most confidence in disposing of current problems would be chosen, and the electorate had alternated its preference between the two very largely on those grounds. Each party had served its country well in former years. Each had at times generated strength and at other times permitted weaknesses to develop within its structure. Furthermore, the rules of the game in United States politics demanded that national elections be carried on without rigid partisan or class appeals, Warren insisted. In that manner the American people would emerge from battle with solidarity rather than division. A more responsive governmental system would result, free of the "retarding influence of bitterness." But for once Earl Warren (and his ticket partner in particular) misjudged the popular pulse. He remained in Sacramento for the time being.

Campaign Style: Caution and Emphasis on the Record

Earl Warren's campaigns for the California governorship laid bare other attributes of his formula for political success. He revealed an obvious aptitude for enunciating cautious and prudent observations intended to alienate as few voters as possible. Yet his pronouncements indicated a knowledge of key state questions and a sincere desire to resolve them; they by no means muzzled an adamant, sometimes ferocious, criticism of the opposition and a ringing self-defense. The Governor persistently tried to steer each verbal exchange toward "the record" in his re-election fights of 1946 and 1950. He was ever hopeful of placing issues and accomplishments "above politics." Crucial to Warren's credo was an abiding faith that a straightforward reiteration of "the facts" was one of the most persuasive of weapons.

The 1942 imbroglio would not qualify as one characterized by sweetness and pacification; the barbs hurled by Oslon and Warren indicated anything but that. Their protracted dispute over civil defense and other matters, the general rancor of Olson's

administration, especially in legislative relations, the ambitions
of an Attorney General accustomed to prosecution and now on
the political offensive for the first significant time in his public
life, were "givens" that year and calculated to produce no little
heat. Warren snapped furiously at the incumbent in many substantive fields. He blamed the Governor for freeing "Communist
radicals" to "curry favor with subversive elements and to win
votes" because the Chief Executive's parole board had released
three men the former Alameda district attorney had sent to
prison for their parts in a 1936 murder. Reciting statistics on the
number of convicts freed since his adversary's inauguration, he
indicted existing parole arrangements as "the darkest chapter in
the Olson administration." The Attorney General told his version
of the civilian defense squabble and accused the Democratic
incumbent of "mishandling" it. He hammered away at the relief
and welfare scandals of the previous few years. He denounced
alleged perversion of the civil service system, specifically pointing a reproachful finger at the dismissal of the Whittier Boys'
School director in favor of a law partner of Olson's Personnel
Board chairman, who supposedly had maneuvered that replace-
ment.[26]

However, Warren's own 1942 platform evinced a real penchant for careful generalization and avoidance of the controversial. His proposals were relatively easy to fulfill and were
attractive to a wide range of California's populace. The would-be
governor "promised" to: make the national emergency his main
preoccupation; work with the legislature, not against it, and
summon special sessions whenever required; give the state guard
and militia every assistance and free them from politics; staff the
Defense Council with experienced men; organize a thorough fire-
prevention system; ask the lawmakers to establish child care
centers; press for a thirty-five-mile speed limit for the duration,
as requested by President Roosevelt; seek ratification of charter
amendments permitting additional cooperation between fire and
police agencies of different cities; subsidize localities when they

---

[26] Burke, *op. cit.*, pp. 220-22; Address at Elks Auditorium, Sacramento,
Aug. 21, 1942, *Warren Speeches*.

undertook certain chores for the state; relax birth-certificate regulations to allow more convenient identification for war jobs; provide compensation to men and women injured in civilian defense duties, until Washington assumed that responsibility; plan for the best use of labor and join the federal government in procuring more out-of-state workers; reduce revenues for non-essential purposes and demand strict economy; create a commission to draft an outline for industrial development and employment after demobilization; restore integrity to merit-system practices; improve old age pensions and urge Sacramento to assume a bigger share of those expenses from the counties; launch a constructive program for rehabilitating prisoners and alter parole stipulations; reconstitute the Fish and Game Commission; pay attention to teachers' retirement measures; and reduce California's sales tax.[27] Incidentally, the 1943 legislature enacted into law all of the points above that called for statutes, except the speed limit.

Warren's circumspection was not confined to reciting his future agenda. He unveiled that trait when attempting to justify his beliefs, even in direct encounters with his antagonist. Olson had almost solid union support, having been endorsed by both the statewide A.F.L. and C.I.O. Warren received very little formal promotion from that sector. His "labor campaign" was spurred principally through the inevitable "auxiliary" associations under the leadership of Charles Real, Oakland Teamster official. The future chief executive's enlistment of sympathy from California's working men and women consisted merely in identifying himself as a charter member of the A.F.L. Musicians' Union, taken out in his boyhood days as a clarinetist in Bakersfield's city band, and in vowing that he had never shown prejudice against them or their organizations. He said: "The right of workers to form unions for collective bargaining upon wages, hours, and conditions of employment is no longer a subject of debate."[28]

---

[27] See especially his summation in the printed copy of his Radio Address, Oct. 30, 1942, *Warren Speeches.*

[28] Address to American Federation of Labor Convention, Aug. 19, 1942, *Warren Speeches.*

Here was harmless phraseology intended to allay possible fears within labor ranks but committing him to nothing specific.

The only personal debate between Warren and Olson, pretty much of a disaster for Warren, was again eloquent testimony to his discretion in expressing himself on certain contentious matters. The encounter concerned a proposition on the November ballot to impose a wartime ban on union "hot cargo" operations and secondary boycotts. Olson objected vehemently to this item. Warren, pressed for his opinion on the subject, confessed: "I am taking a neutral position on the hot cargo bill because I believe it is absolutely imperative that bitterness and controversy should be avoided at this time on any issue which tends to divide our people. . . . The question is on the referendum ballot—in the hands of the highest authority in this state, the voters of California—and in this period of grave crisis, it should not be made a political football in the governorship campaign."[29]

These artful exercises in circumlocution did not deter Warren from vigorously extolling his public stewardship and briskly repulsing assaults on it. When not chiding Kenny on legislative relations or on the package deal in 1946, his statements then were essentially reviews of the measures he had put forth during his first term. The 1950 gubernatorial campaign also exemplified Warren's penchant for elaboration upon his stewardship at the capitol and reciting "the facts." He was assisted in that regard by Democratic rival James Roosevelt, who went to greater lengths than Kenny in throwing down the gauntlet to the Governor on substantive issues. However, there the dissimilarity to 1946 ends. Roosevelt too made periodic allusions to party devotion and he was able to present little that was contrary to Warren's policy agenda. Nevertheless, Roosevelt received from Warren a more stinging rebuke than had Kenny, although he was generally treated less harshly than Oslon.

The 1950 Democratic aspirant disparaged the administration's record on highway, school, and housing construction. He particularly scolded the incumbent for not devoting enough state

---

[29] Remarks to San Francisco Forum, Oct. 11, 1942, *Warren Speeches*.

money to the aged and unemployed. Warren jibed at his opponent's fiscal irresponsibility, declaring that a balance must be
struck between level of service and available cash. He once
charged: "Mr. Roosevelt's promises are just so many rubber
checks issued against a something-for-nothing bank account. In
due time those checks would bounce!"[30] The Governor rapped
Roosevelt for "unconscionable glibness" in holding out hope of
lower revenue rates at the same time. The Democrat had suggested that the Chief Executive's pet $75,000,000 "rainy day" fund,
so painstakingly laid away as a cushion against severe recession,
might do nicely as a source of immediate capital. Warren
countered: "Roosevelt has spent this same seventy-five million
dollars over and over again—for pensions in Northern California,
for highways in the Sierras, for power projects in the Central
Valley—for every local project at the places he stops."[31]

The two men traded some of their heaviest punches on the
state's explosive education issue. Roosevelt taunted the Governor
for lack of accomplishment in that field. Warren's rebuttal was a
reiteration of the number of enterprises undertaken and dollars
donated to schools and colleges during his administration. The
ranting of his antagonist should come as no shock, Warren
scoffed, for as this heir of great wealth had attended private
academic institutions all of his life, he could scarcely be expected
to have much grasp of *public* needs in this field. Warren ful-
minated: "Recognizing that he is suffering from a complete lack
of campaign issues, he has tried to manufacture one regarding
public schools, but I still marvel at the effrontery of a political
opportunist possessed of the gall to ignore the fact that since I
have been governor new public school construction programs
have provided facilities in our elementary and high schools for
600,000 pupils."[32]

Roosevelt inveighed lustily against Warren on the topic of
employment. He charged that the Governor had ignored many

---

[30] Radio Address, May 26, 1950, *Warren Speeches.*

[31] Address to Rally at Scottish Rite Temple, San Francisco, June 2,
1950, *Warren Speeches.*

[32] *Ibid.*

suggestions for ameliorating joblessness and he advocated a state agency to attract new industry. Warren's rejoinder was: "I wonder if you have noticed that most of the time Mr. Roosevelt is not making fantastic promises he is acting in the role of prophet of doom. Time after time, he has said we have one-half million unemployed and implied that we are on our way to one million unemployed. Once again I want to give you some facts."[33] The number idled in California, Warren said, stood at 374,000 on April 15 of that year, a figure which also counted persons switching jobs and those who had recently moved into the state and were still looking for work. While his sympathies went to people who were off the payrolls, he and his subordinates were doing something about the problem through public works and other enterprises. Besides, the April, 1950, total was quite a reduction from the early postwar peak of 531,000 and represented 103,000 fewer unemployed than on that same date the previous year. Warren admonished: "These are facts and figures which should make any prophet of doom hold his head in shame. Mr. Roosevelt and his extremist cohorts have been talking about a million unemployed so long that I am sure they will never be satisfied unless we have it. . . . They believe they could then profit politically on distress."[34]

Warren gave Roosevelt another tongue lashing on the subject of employment. In this instance he again showed a talent for making political capital of Democratic rhetoric. His remarks contained more than a tinge of irony, considering the personalities involved: "Mr. Roosevelt, who bears the distinction of being the first candidate for governor of California to reveal on the official ballot that he has no occupation, has deliberately assumed the role of prophet of doom. There was once a President who said that in this country we have nothing to fear but fear itself. Yet we have in our midst a political opportunist who apparently believes that this utterance is not in keeping with true American philosophy. He has gone about the state deliberately using

---

33 Radio Address, May 26, 1950, *Warren Speeches.*
34 *Ibid.*

language designed to promote fear among the people. At a time when every state is marvelling at our economic progress he is telling the people we are headed toward breadlines and an early return to the dole. With extravagance born of desperation he promised to wave a magic wand and do away with all unemployment. He doesn't tell us how nor can he tell us how. Actually, when you pin him down he says 'me too' to all those programs which we utilized to keep California in the forefront of employment."[35]

Warren's most fervent defense of his record against Roosevelt's diatribes was made in the area of aid to the aged. The Democrat grumbled that arrangements for subsidies to the elderly were "in confusion because we have lacked clear-sighted and bold leadership in the present state government."[36] Roosevelt embraced most of the ideas espoused by California's celebrated pension promoter, George McLain. McLain's novel thoughts on the subject were voted into law in November, 1948, only to be erased one year later (much to Warren's delight). Specifically, the Democratic candidate wanted outright state direction and the elimination of county functions in that field, removal of relatives' responsibility, liberalization of personal-property limitations, restoration to eligibility of the sixty-three- and sixty-four-year age groups whose payments had been cut off by the popular revocation of McLain's setup, and minimum allowances of seventy-five dollars monthly. In the long run, said Roosevelt, "we should aim at a benefit of at least one hundred dollars per person a month, tied to a realistic cost-of-living scale."[37]

Warren left few stones unturned in trying to link his opponent to McLain. He dubbed the pension advocate "an unsavory character who has lived off the recipients of old-age assistance without doing an honest day's work in years." These two comrades in arms, he said, were preaching something that could not then be delivered in size of grants. Indeed, they were trudging the

---

[35] Address to Political Rally, June 2, 1950, *Warren Speeches.*
[36] *Los Angeles Times,* Apr. 16, 1950, p. 34.
[37] *Ibid.*

length and breadth of California and implying that only if the
sitting governor were ousted could the prevailing maximum even
be retained. The Chief Executive's disclaimer was sharply
couched: "It is an insidious attempt to poison the minds of . . .
citizens who are totally dependent for their living on these pensions. It is not only untrue, it is cruel beyond description to
terrorize people in these circumstances. In their joint bid for
political power, Mr. Roosevelt and Mr. McLain care nothing for
the peace of mind of these elderly people or for the stability of
our state. They are willing to set group against group, and even
destroy confidence in the government itself. . . ."[38]

The Governor's blood pressure rose sharply when he received
a pathetic letter from a widowed aid recipient. She recounted
her hardships and then asked Warren if it was true that he would
diminish the maximum payment from seventy-five to sixty-five
dollars if he were re-elected, as had been implied during the
campaign. Warren snapped: "My answer to her and all in her
situation is that it is a deliberate falsehood—maliciously designed
with two purposes in mind—one, to discredit me in the eyes of
the elder citizens; and second, to further the money-making
scheme of McLain which can only flourish through the generating
of fear and frustration among the elderly of our state."[39]

Warren noted that he had approved the concept of public
assistance to senior citizens "long before George McLain ever
conceived the idea of shaving his living off the pension payments of older citizens." He reminded his constituents that in
1926 he had even welcomed a plan for helping the elderly drawn
up by the Fraternal Order of Eagles. Since then it had not been
the George McLains who advanced their cause. It was, instead,
the earnest people, like himself, "who recognize the unhappy
plight of many of our older citizens in a highly industralized
economy and who recognize the obligation of society to those
who have contributed to the up-building of our state through
their productive years—only to be thrust aside by more or less

[38] Radio Address, May 31, 1950, *Warren Speeches.*
[39] *Ibid.*

arbitrary age limits for employment. I have always been for pensions, and for liberalizations of pensions, as a matter of right."[40]

Characteristically, Warren endeavored to place the whole question "above politics." He felt that "the quickest and surest way to jeopardize old age security is to have the pension issue become a football of politics. The quickest and surest way to bring heartache and worry and insecurity to older citizens is to have the pension program fall into the clutches of scheming politicians and self-seeking demagogues. In all parts of our state, these two apostles of fear and foreboding have been spreading the gospel of impending doom. They don't deal in facts or figures because to tell the truth would ruin their entire scheme. Let's look at the facts."[41]

The Governor said that California was then investing twice as much to subsidize the elderly as any other state. More persons were so reimbursed than in New York and Pennsylvania combined, although those two states had an aggregate population more than double that of California. Furthermore, California's aid recipients could possess up to twelve hundred dollars in cash and personal property and hold title to their own homes. True, the state did have a relatives'-responsibility clause in its code; however, those in lesser income brackets were relieved of much of the burden of sustaining their parents. Finally, the top subvention had risen from forty to seventy-five dollars monthly during his governorship. Warren concluded: "We increased it because we could afford to finance the increases. The pensioners have been paid in dollars, not pie-in-the-sky."[42] Partly in tribute to an astute defense of his official record, the electorate in 1950 returned Warren to the capitol by a landslide for a third time.

Thus Warren displayed an unusually deft reliance on a strategy of nonpartisanship in campaigning for the California governorship. He shrewdly projected the image of a public servant dedicated to personal accountability and given to forthrightness.

---

40 *Ibid.*
41 *Ibid.*
42 *Ibid.*

He was most cognizant of the "temper of the time" and a "sense of the possible" in the state's current political milieu. Indeed, he showed an alert recognition of those basic mores of the American democratic order that enjoin too drastic an appeal in vote hunting and abet those of more moderate tone. For those reasons Republican Earl Warren lived not merely to fight another day but endured for nearly eleven years as the longest-tenured governor in a state heavily Democratic by registration. Yet his bipartisan guise was by no means simply an electioneering gimmick. He put it into practice in dispatching governmental business. It was quite evident in the type of advice he solicited in formulating programs for presentation to the legislature.

CHAPTER III

Earl Warren: Executive Policymaker

In times past, standard thought in American politics had it that policymaking was virtually coterminous with lawmaking. Our legislative bodies supposedly dominated governmental program development, leaving to the executive the implementation of public projects and to the courts the interpretation of the laws upon which they were based. Yet as time passed it became increasingly apparent that the process of shaping official courses of action is much more of a continuum that encompasses legislative, administrative, judicial, and electoral phases. The "separation of powers" doctrine today plays a role secondary to its vital twin "checks and balances." The three branches, plus a host of nongovernmental forces exerted mainly through interest groups and political parties, are all involved, in ever shifting degrees, in fixing the agenda of public business.

Certainly an obvious trend is the ever growing and sometimes all-pervasive power of the executive in the policymaking cycle, although it is rivaled of late by a willful judiciary. In most jurisdictions the chief executive is picked by all the voters and not by segments of the electorate as are the bulk of our legislators. Publicity and mass attention are fixed on him. He has a growing command of the data and expertise so crucial to the construction of complicated proposals of state. For these reasons, chief executives across the country now have one of the most potent hands, if not always the strongest hand, in governmental procedures generally and in legislative doings in particular. However, in many states and localities they must share authority and a part of the limelight with a bevy of other popularly chosen administrators. This is true in California, where the governor's span of control is reduced by the independent election of such officers as secretary of state, controller, attorney general, treasurer, superintendent of public instruction, and the board of equalization, in addition to the lieutenant governor. The state constitution says that the governor shall have *"supreme executive power"* (italics mine);[1] all the rest is scattered and lodged elsewhere.

One exhaustive study concludes that a governor's policy concerns overlap three areas: administrative, legislative, and partisan. He wears three hats, as head administrator, legislative leader, and party chieftain.[2] Still, most chief executives tend to blur this trilogy in their daily performance. In those few states with a relatively even two-party balance and a modicum of discipline at the polls, such intertwining is accepted as part of the natural order of the universe. There partisan planks are frequently cardinal components in the gubernatorial list of pursuits. In strict or modified one-party jurisdictions a different mix occurs. Here normal partisanship is all but absent, since there is no healthy cross-party challenge. In such places the governor's plans are conditioned only faintly by Republican or Democratic pronouncements and are inclined to be personal in tone. Neither in officeholding nor in registration did California conform to the two-party pattern during Warren's terms in Sacramento. It was heavily Republican in the first instance, abundantly Democratic in the second. This ironic dichotomy coaxed most Republican aspirants and incumbents, Earl Warren among them, into forswearing close partisan ties if their lease on public life was to run for long.

Program Development, Warren Style

Warren recognized that both administrative and legislative sectors weighed mightily in the ultimate fruition of most policies. Yet given the state's political milieu then and his own nonpartisan

---

[1] California Constitution (1879), Art. 5, Sec. 1.

[2] Coleman Ransone, *The Office of Governor in the United States* (Birmingham: Univ. of Alabama Press, 1956), p. 157.

predilections, he was less inclined than many American governors to wear the party hat as a policymaker. Thus the Governor put little trust in Republican party officials per se for opinions on bills to be sponsored by his administration. This is not to say that persons who fitted the description of Republican or Democratic "stalwart" were never consulted. One can be both party leader and subject-matter professional, a truism the Chief Executive fully appreciated; nonetheless, he sought the views of his informants for their content values and tried to suppress in his own mind whatever partisan overtones those views might contain.

The President of the United States and most governors have several well-known sources of information at their disposal for developing programs. Their immediate staffs, line-executive departments, legislators and their research agencies, interest-group spokesmen, and party functionaries, are all available. California's Earl Warren not only put to use each of these wellsprings of advice, excepting the partisan, but added some new twists to the procedure of idea accumulation. Desirous of maximum co-ordination between legislature and administration, he frequently asked little bands of lawmakers to meet with him and his sub-ordinates prior to the opening gavel in assembly and senate to discuss possible statutory objectives. Solons of both major political persuasions with marked interest and competence in particular areas were asked to take the lead in drafting and managing the fate of administration items. As the sessions wore on, Republican and Democratic legislators whose chores bore materially on the fortunes of gubernatorial proposals were invited over for talks. In these exchanges the Governor presented his case in friendly, give-and-take style, employing a personal rather than a partisan appeal. Members of both houses were vigorous participants in the citizen advisory bodies Warren mobilized from time to time to propose planks for his platforms.

Nor was Warren reluctant to hear observations from groups with axes to grind on given questions, although he generally refused to commit himself to specifics. Anxious to launch state compulsory health insurance in 1945, he sat down in December, 1944, with Dr. Phillip K. Gilman, president-elect of the California

Medical Association, to outline his proposition. He assured the physician that it would bring about no interference with the doctor-patient relationship. Gilman convened the C.M.A.'s executive committee for a luncheon with the Governor at the Sutter Club, where the Governor once again expounded upon the merits of his plan and asked assistance in putting it across. He and his aides also contacted state Federation of Labor and Chamber of Commerce representatives on the subject. Many features of his 1945 measure resulted from these interchanges. However, it took the C.M.A. House of Delegates only a few days to denounce Warren's project. This response foreshadowed the furious hostility of that organization which would ultimately help to scuttle the enterprise in the legislature.

The Governor nearly always kept the State Federation posted when putting labor bills on assembly and senate desks, and even sponsored a measure written almost exclusively by that organization. Most of the stipulations in his 1946 overture for sickness and disability payments under unemployment compensation originated with the labor body. Yet Warren always insisted upon reserving final decisions for himself on any request sent to him by a private interest, after wide-ranging discussions in the group realm.

The Citizen Advisory Bodies

With great regularity the President and many state chief executives now lean on the counsel of sundry "citizen advisory" units—agglomerations either of massive lay membership or of restricted dimension composed of experts, or a combination of both. They are used not only for programmatic thoughts but for general support and favorable public relations as well. Differing sizes and shapes of conferences, committees, councils, and task forces have long been a feature of the national scene. Their subjects have encompassed child betterment, education, natural resources and conservation, health, problems of the aging, highway improvement, air transportation, phases of law enforcement, civil rights, employment, aspects of foreign affairs, and aid to depressed areas, to cite a brief list. Indeed, some of the citizen bodies formed in California during the Warren years worked closely with those at the federal level. The Governor's Mid-Century Conference on Children and Youth in September of 1950 was technically a subordinate branch of a national symposium held that same year under Harry Truman. Their composite recommendations appeared under the same cover. The Chief Executive's two 1946 traffic-safety confabs were held just prior to and immediately following a similar convocation in Washington under the auspices of the national Democratic administration. Along with purely local goals, the second California parley was designed to implement the national program in the state.

Warren's advocacy of mandatory medical insurance starting in 1945 and his championship of numerous other advances in public and mental health thereafter furnished background material for President Truman's 1948 national health assembly and for the subsequent presidential commission on the health needs of the nation. The nationwide turmoil over government hospital and doctor protection during the Fair Deal years from 1948 to 1952 was in a sense a direct consequence of a similar clash between California's chief executive and its medical society. This clash commenced in 1945, continued for several years, and merged with the polemics at the higher level. The two fights featured analogous program specifics; each saw the famed California campaign-management firm of Whitaker and Baxter take the side of the physicians and surgeons. President Truman's migratory labor commission was initiated in June, 1950, and carried on for about a year. It started its inquiry soon after Warren's Committee to Survey the Agricultural Resources of the San Joaquin Valley was launched. The two entities exchanged thoughts and gave each other general encouragement during that time.

Earl Warren was something of an innovator in that he drew greater sustenance from these consultative bodies for suggested policies and popular backing than most of his counterparts around the country. Certainly he put them to more extensive use than did his predecessors or successors in California. The

Governor was cognizant of the state's heterogeneous makeup and
of the tremendous diversity of economic and social thought with
in its borders. In a place like California no one segment of the
populace could possibly monopolize all valid ideas requisite to
generating governmental movement and resolving public prob
lems. Thus Warren searched tirelessly for a broad base of "part
nership" with his constituents. He tried consciously to secure
some voice, however limited, for almost all sectors of society in
the policy-forming process. In this way he armed himself with
data crucial to his business agenda. He also won vital political
friendship which he, as an affiliated Republican in a state with a
superabundance of Democratic registrants, could not have at
tained had he listened solely to his GOP brethren or to his own
internal administration in Sacramento.

For these reasons the Chief Executive made distinctive use
of conferences, committees, and commissions to probe state
issues. Not only were these groups of dedicated people composed
of men and women from all walks of life, they were picked irres
pective of partisan credentials. Here was another facet of
Warren's brand of nonpartisanship. Because party platforms
were often more nebulous in California than elsewhere, official
proposals had to be forged very largely in the furnaces of in
dividual officeholders and private interests. Said the Governor
about his 1943 unit to study old age stipends: "The committee
now being appointed, constituting as it does a cross-section of
the pension thought of the state, should be able to eliminate
those political considerations which have so often confused dis
cussions of pension matters. . . ."[3] What better way was there to
plumb group opinion and still control the outcome to a degree?
What superior method to stimulate that unity so cherished by
the Governor? Indeed, what better manner to satiate his prag
matic appetite for thorough digestion of the facts?

The conferences were far larger and more of a medley in
composition. Sixteen of these gatherings published reports or

---

[3] California Legislature, 55th Sess., *Assembly Journal*, Apr. 10, 1943
(Sacramento: 1943), pp. 1954-55.

ten different topics throughout Warren's governorship. They dealt with educational television, employment, industrial safety, mental health, old age, senile patients, sex crimes against children, traffic safety, water, and youth and child welfare. The committees and commissions differed in several respects from the conferences. They were more engrossed with detailed preparation of suggested actions than were the conferences, although both served that purpose. The commissions and committees were smaller and more continuous in nature, ranging in membership from five to seventeen and ordinarily functioning for a number of months. The bigger conclaves usually endured but for a day or two, in some instances with over two thousand persons on the roster. The smaller units consisted of individuals of specialized background, being less of a cross section of the state's inhabitants than were the conferences. Twelve of these smaller groups reported on the subjects of agricultural labor, civil disturbances, crime, old age pensions, penal affairs, postwar problems, and taxation. In effect, many advisory bodies functioned as bipartisan gubernatorial pressure groups in the legislative process, working to bring to fruition proposals of theirs which the Governor had incorporated in his program.

The commissions and committees proved their worth most in terms of deep study and concrete policy alternatives. While the conferences were valuable in that way as well, they probably were of greater utility as arenas for comprehensive debate among people of diversified viewpoint in developing mass consensus on key issues. The Governor told his 1949 employment conferees: "I have called this meeting today in the spirit of the town meeting because I believe we need an exchange of ideas. . . . [The conference] should provide an opportunity for a frank scrutiny of California's employment and unemployment problems, for a full exploration of the best possible answers, and can lead to concerted action in the communities. . . . It is my firm belief that when the people's government provides a forum for the examination of a problem, action by the people themselves will follow. We have merely tried to bring together the leaders of our state to dissect the employment problem, and then put it back together in a manner which will stimulate community action in creating and maintaining jobs."[4]

Thus the larger conclaves had as one sweeping purpose the alerting of popular attention to state public affairs. They also spurred citizen reflection and performance, building confidence that the task could be done through private or local efforts if Sacramento's operations were impeded for any reason. After adjournment of the 1951 confab on the elderly, its chairman wrote that "one of the most stimulating things about the conference has been its aftereffects. The enthusiasm generated has carried over into positive community follow-up. . . . More than twenty California communities . . . have held meetings to discuss ways and means of effectuating conference recommendations and in initiating local programs for their senior citizens. This speaks well for our civic consciousness. . . ."[5] Civic dedication aside, these parleys were most profitable in constructing broad, bipartisan affection for Warren's administration.

The Chief Executive doubtless won other points in the political game through these huge gatherings. To be sure, they satisfied his desire for unity among California's manifold interests. To him, this was manatory to a meaningful attack on existing problems. Beyond that, and trite and old-fashioned as it may sound, he was an ardent believer in mass participation in government and a staunch advocate of balanced representation. He told his 1945 water parley: "Its purpose is to provide an opportunity for the people of California to place their thoughts on record. . . . Naturally . . . many points of view will arise. It is my hope that the conference will lay the foundation for reconciling divergent views, and that it will result in an overall program that will aid each community to grow and prosper. We must . . . attempt to reach a common ground of understanding and compromise. On such a basis, apparently conflicting developments—

---

[4] *Proceedings of the Governor's Conference on Employment*, Dec. 5-6, 1949 (Sacramento: 1950), pp. 11-12.

[5] Cited in the opening address of the Governor, *Proceedings of the Governor's Conference on the Problems of the Aging*, Oct. 15-16, 1951 (Sacramento: 1951), p. 10.

each meritorious in its own right—may be brought to fruition without loss or damage to others. It is my hope that through this open discussion of our water problems, a program may be developed for the guidance of the legislative and administrative branches of your state government that will achieve the highest degree of equity and usefulness."[6] In the Governor's words the surmise is hinted at that by inviting expression from almost every portion of state society, those whose pet panaceas were turned down would feel somewhat more inclined to go along with the ultimate solution agreed upon, simply because they were a part of the prior decision-making.

It was rare indeed for Warren to pledge *carte blanche* acceptance of all suggestions emerging from one of the conferences. Still, he did generally associate himself with the final reports turned out by such groups. By doing so, he linked himself with what was presumably bipartisan and majority opinion in the given areas—an astute political ploy, if nothing else. By granting a day in court to persons who were not exactly his favorites of the moment, not only might their antagonism be lessened but their effectiveness in winning later sympathy for their own nostrums could by substantially curtailed. The Governor could then merely point out that they had been graciously asked to come to Sacramento to partake of a free and democratic exchange, only to depart as ingrates complaining because their own selfish dogmas had not been accepted. Warren took great pains to give an impression of fair play in his handling of these meetings. He conveyed the image of an administrator willing to listen with keen interest and an open mind to nearly any kind of proposition. This did him no harm at election time.

Such broader goals notwithstanding, both basic varieties of citizen advisory bodies turned out a multitude of worthwhile policy recommendations. Many of them found their way into gubernatorial legislative pronouncements and eventually California's laws. Warren sometimes incorporated into his messages

---

[6] From prefatory statement to *Proceedings of the California Water Conference*, Dec. 6-7, 1945 (Sacramento: 1946).

to the lawmakers all or most of the judgments made by these battalions of conscientious individuals. This he did either by outright endorsement or by generally commending a given report to the assembly and the senate. However, tangible output was less clear at other times. Examination of the Governor's proposals to the legislature discloses that numerically only a small percentage of total findings by these groups seems to have had a reasonably direct connection with his plans. This fact is explained partly by the Chief Executive's penchant for the nonspecific in program espousal, a trait examined further in the next chapter, on legislative relations. Furthermore, that same characteristic was manifested by many of the conferences, commissions, and committees. All of their publications together comprised several thousand assertions, with a big proportion couched in general terms. Many suggestions were aimed directly at the legislators and did not seem to invite executive intervention. A number were intended for local governments; still others asked private enterprise to do certain things. Thus on comparatively few items was the Governor moved to comment further. Nonetheless, several noteworthy measures backed by certain citizen units were later promoted by Warren.

Only once, after his 1949 conclave on sex crimes, did Warren subscribe to all requests made by a conference. Recounting the group's declarations before an extraordinary legislative session, he agreed "that these provisions are desirable and I urge your consideration of them. . . ."[7] It was more common for the Governor to take favorable note of the outcome of deliberations, thank his guests for their convictions and for the exhilarating effect their endeavors had on his administration, and promise his continued interest. His observations on the outcome of his 1951 parley on the aging were typical: "Now I don't propose to comment on any of the recommendations that have been made by you although I agree with many of them without any further study. All I say to you is that we will study each and every one

---

[7] *Message to the California Legislature of December 12, 1949* (Sacramento: 1949), p. 4.

of these recommendations, that we will make this subject a major item of our administration, and we will try with your help to solve the problems of the aging to the best of our ability."[8]

Warren gave his consent in that manner to a number of ideas advanced by several conferences, notably that on employment in 1949, that on mental health the same year, that on the complications of old age in 1951, and that called in 1950 to study the difficulties faced by senile patients. His ensuing speeches before the lawmakers were on many points in fundamental agreement with earlier statements by these assemblages. In the field of labor and job procurement these items encompassed, among other things, passage of a fair employment practices statute; higher benefits under jobless-disability and industrial-accident compensation, and their extension to agricultural workers and other classes not then covered; alteration of California's employer "merit rating" system; approval of compulsory health insurance, a matter on which Warren was in great need of all moral and political support that could be gathered; and provision for state economic planning.

The Governor agreed with his mental health advisers on numerous propositions, including those to establish a new community-services division in the mental hygiene department, expand mental hospitals, construct diagnostic and acute-treatment centers in five state facilities, increase institutional personnel, and assist in creating psychiatric wards in county general hospitals. Also proposed were the building of two alcoholic-therapy units, one above the Tehachapi Mountains and the other in the Southland, and the construction of a home for mental defectives in the Los Angeles region. The Governor stood squarely behind the conference that investigated the problems of the elderly on at least two key recommendations: first, the necessity for legal formation of a continuing citizen committee to inspire community ventures in that sphere, and second, the need to raise the pension maximum again. He also approved the construction of county-operated special dispensaries for senile care, with costs

---

[8] *Proceedings of Governor's Conference on Aging,* p. 263.

to be shared by Sacramento, a measure suggested by the preceding conference on that topic.

The transactions of his more compact and usually more proficient committees and commissions were most persuasive with the Governor in shaping statutory objectives. Here he borrowed for personal presentation to California's solons every stipulation of three such groups—his 1943 body on taxation, the 1943 panel on old age pensions, and his 1943 investigatory unit on penal affairs. The Chief Executive praised most propositions advanced by the remaining committees and commissions. His compliments about the committee report on San Joaquin Valley agricultural workers and other matters is illustrative here; he told the assemblymen and senators: "It points the way to sensible and needed changes in the laws governing the operations of labor contractors and the inspection of farm labor housing. It deals with the welfare, health, and educational aspects of the problem. I am sure you will be able to use it as the basis for correcting many of the undersirable conditions. . . ."[9] Warren's later remarks to the two legislative chambers were highly similar to the language used in the account made by the farm-labor unit. Both wanted to tighten regulations and standards for labor contractors and worker camps, while increasing the enforcement staff of California's industrial relations department in the process, to provide unemployment insurance and low-interest home loans for agricultural employees, to furnish state underwriting for counties that aided these people, and to give additional protection to children doing farm chores.

Obvious accord existed between the Governor and his committees and commissions in the spheres of crime, old age pensions, postwar reconstruction and reconversion, and taxation. He echoed his criminal fact-finding units in asking for a law to require periodic crime surveys in each county by the attorney general, and legislation to outlaw draw poker and other forms of gambling. They agreed that California needed a statute to revoke the license of any business that tolerated the use or sale

---

[9] *Inaugural Address of January 8, 1951* (Sacramento: 1951), p. 9.

of narcotics, catered to B-girls, or was hospitable to what is known jokingly in some circles as the quadruple P—panderers, perverts, pimps, and prostitutes. Warren and his citizen bodies in this field also wanted to strengthen tax codes as a weapon to combat organized crime, launch a new administrative unit to look into evasion of revenue statutes, and build two state hospitals for treatment of alcoholics.

The Chief Executive felt that his 1943 committee probing old age pensions had valuable ideas in seeking to elevate the stipend maximum from forty to fifty dollars monthly, raise the permitted value of real estate owned from three thousand to thirty-five hundred dollars for husband and wife, up personal-property limitations from five hundred to six hundred dollars per person, continue relatives' responsibility, and continue county administration of public assistance under state supervision, with modifications in the contributory scale of relatives' responsibility and with the state's assumption of one half the local share of subventions to needy aged.

Warren borrowed freely for his own platforms a variety of planks furnished by his Reconstruction and Re-Employment Commission on the encompassing subject of reconversion, some of the same notions being reflected in the reports of other bodies too. In line with their final transcripts, he asked the lawmakers for many things. He requested additional money for the postwar employment reserve and highway construction. He asked them to reduce the 5 percent interest rate on veterans' home and farm purchases, to reorganize California's military and veterans' affairs department, and to widen apprentice, on-the-job, and vocational training for returning servicemen. He hoped the solons would enlarge and improve state public health services to localities, build new facilities for youngsters with cerebral palsy, conduct a survey to determine the number of hospitals needed in the postwar period, and enact compulsory medical insurance. The assembly and the senate were also advised to extend unemployment benefits to firms with a single employee (down from those with four on the payroll) and to agricultural laborers, domestics, public servants, and workers in nonprofit corporations, and to liberalize the system to encompass jobless-disability grants. Other points of mutual legislative interest to Warren and his advisers included a statewide program of general public assistance administered through counties under state surveillance, a yearly "production and employment estimate," new state agencies on fair employment practices and industrial relations, a master airport plan, and a new state aviation commission.

The Chief Executive associated himself completely with the findings of his 1943 tax-inquiry body, a committee named specifically to make recommendations to him and the legislators regarding the entire revenue structure in California. He petitioned the lawmakers to honor its pleas to retire certain bond issues, inaugurate a $25,000,000 war-catastrophe fund, make available some $33,000,000 more for state construction, and lower a number of revenues by specific figures and durations. The last item would allow a reduction in sales levies, boost personal-income exemptions, and lessen the burden of bank and corporation franchise and corporate-earnings assessments.

The Official Family

The California governor, like other state heads and the President, also leans heavily upon an army of civil servants and his own appointees for aspects of policy elaboration. Most popularly elected chief executives must secure in their administrations both over-all quality and responsiveness to the public will. Exertions in these directions are compelled at the state level by the expanding scope and increasing intricacy of present problems, prevalent for some time nationally. Complicated organizational, procedural, and substantive decisions involving medical science, labor benefits, social welfare measures, public works, planning, conservation and resource development, and a host of other problems call for the daily application of specialized talents. However, such programs do entail nontechnical determinations as well. They are matters of vital concern to ordinary citizens, whose interests are constantly at stake in the judgments of the experts. Therefore, ranking officers must somehow recruit a staff that is trained and competent, yet attuned to wide-ranging human needs.

One principal task of the American governor is to furnish comprehensive guidance and coordination. He must balance many specialized demands upon the financial resources and energies of the state. The voters often find it difficult to evaluate policy specifics, although they can assess the broad results of an administration. Through the responsible elected officials they then render a periodic verdict at the ballot box. Thus of all powers held by a chief executive, probably none is more fundamental nor politically more revelant over the long run than choosing immediate subordinates and spurring them and their dependent bureaucracies to proficient and faithful performance. Prolonged and successful endurance in any governorship is largely dependent on wise use of that authority.

Restrictions on gubernatorial appointments in California are familiar. They include legal or constitutional requirements that some principal nominees submit to the "advise and consent" of the senate; that technical qualifications to be met by applicants for given posts be spelled out; and that time periods for length of duty be fixed, thereby restricting the governor because some remain in his service for unalterable durations and not at his pleasure. Yet no restraint on his unfettered choice of personnel is so pervasive as the widespread use of the merit principle. Virtually all major California administrative units are under civil service, often up to and including the post of deputy director. The governor's appointing prerogative is exercised mainly in drafting department directors, some of their immediate deputies, and the membership of the countless boards and commissions which dot California's executive branch. Yet Earl Warren hardly considered the state's generous merit arrangements a drawback. He was a consistent and diligent champion of the system both before and during his governorship, for it perfectly suited his nonpartisan ideology and his desire for professional fact-finding. Indeed, he helped draft the voter-pamphlet argument in the successful 1934 campaign to expand the system and insert its provisions into the state constitution.

The new Chief Executive expressed his views on the subject shortly after his inauguration, briefly restirring the ashes from his 1942 pyrrhic clash with Olson: "I intend to restore civil service to its proper place in state government. . . . There must be no discrimination or preference shown employees because of their political affiliation. . . . Employees shall not be solicited for campaign funds for state officers. . . . There is not going to be any more juggling of eligible lists in order to bring about the appointment of political favorites. . . ."[10] The Governor's faith in the program was manifest in his subsequent actions, for the adult authority, the prisons, the public-utilities commission, and the justice department were all later brought under the system with an ardent push from him.

Nationally and in many states there exists what some would call another limitation on the chief executive's unbridled right to pick his prime aides—a temptation to cater to the political party. In Washington at any one time virtually the entire cabinet and the bulk of sub-cabinet positions are filled with those of the same partisan designation as the President, with isolated exceptions. In contrast, partisan factors were given short shrift by Warren in appointing people to executive jobs in California, because of the independent political atmosphere and his own proneness to individualism. Republicans were predominant among his agency heads; yet Democrats also served. Subject-matter fitness and administrative aptitude without regard to partisanship were uppermost in the Governor's mind in selecting each of his subordinates. Perhaps his most lasting contribution in this realm was a concerted and generally successful attempt to professionalize state departmental directorships, a tradition of expertise so ingrained by the time of his move to the national Supreme Court that his successors saw no reason to alter it. The profusion of boards and commissions that abound in California's governmental landscape gave Warren still another opportunity to reward not the party loyal but qualified persons of either persuasion who might have boosted him politically.

10 *Sacramento Bee,* Dec. 22, 1942, p. 1.

The President and American governors ordinarily take other ingredients into account in completing their corps of advisers. Geographic location, group identifications, and personal loyalty are all weighed and a balance is struck. While Warren was cognizant of these other requisites for high public employment, he was different in the degree with which he studiously tried to eschew partisan connections and to exalt substantive knowledge and managerial ability. When first naming his principal associates in 1943, he pointed to them with pride: "They are men and women who have spent their lives perfecting themselves for high service and that is the qualification I am searching for as I proceed with the creation of the official family."[11] His legislative secretary told me that the Governor was hard put (and probably not embarrassed) to list the political ties of several of his major subordinates in one of his early press conferences.[12] He was more concerned that "everyone appointed can and will make an honest, forceful and healthy effort to render nonpartisan service to the people."[13]

The Chief Executive searched diligently for individuals who would meet his high standards for the positions in question. It risks understatement to say that all prospects were exhaustively screened. A folder of information on each post was maintained in the Governor's office. Materials bearing upon the past and present status of every job were kept on one side of the file. Included were such things as data on the current incumbent and any expiration date for his term, backgrounds and descriptions of tours of duty for those who had held the job earlier, and supporting items. All correspondence relative to the future of that job was chronicled on the opposite side of the file. Requests from aspirants, both serious and crackpot, dossiers on the more legitimate ones compiled by the gubernatorial staff, letters from

---

[11] Speech to California New Press Association Luncheon, San Francisco, Jan. 16, 1943, *Warren Speeches.*

[12] Hon. Beach Vasey (R), judge of the Superior Court of Los Angeles County, former legislative secretary to Gov. Warren. Interview, May 3, 1956.

[13] News Press speech.

assorted pressures plugging some worthy, and other relevant data were found there. An appointments secretary kept this documentation up to date and briefed Warren on forthcoming openings, each of which the Governor discussed thoroughly with his principal aides when the appropriate time arrived.

Warren was acting in accord with common practice around the country when he invited help, as he frequently did, from the private groups most directly affected by the work of a given agency in picking its ranking officers. He made it a habit to consult the State Federation on assignments available in the labor sphere. He was an originator of unique procedures in this area too. He started a ritual imitated, albeit more sporadically, by his successors: the submission of all judicial hopefuls to the state bar association, even though that was not mandatory by law. He announced candidly that any lawyer would have to "run the gauntlet of his own profession" before receiving his blessing for a coveted court seat: "if he cannot come through after an investigation by his own profession as being qualified for the bench, he will not be appointed to any judicial position."[14] He looked to the judiciary and to the lawyers for instruction in forming selective-service and appeal boards during World War II, a task turned over to the states by Washington. Once again he came up with a totally new method. The nomination of local members was delegated to superior-court judges in the county, appellate justices submitted names for the higher bodies, and the bar proposed appeal agents. Warren boasted later that he had accepted each suggestion made and had received no complaints that reflected on the personnel presiding over the draft machinery.

Warren was naturally actuated by geography and sectionalism, especially in a big and diverse state like California, in staffing his departments. Sixteen directors who worked under him during his nearly eleven years in Sacramento could be indentified as Southlanders because of their earlier pursuits (if not by birth,

---

[14] Address to the California State Bar Association, Aug. 4, 1943, *Warren Speeches.*

since natives were a comparative rarity even then). The Los Angeles metropolitan area had by far the biggest representation among the southerners. Fifteen were northerners, emanating primarily from the San Francisco Bay region and secondarily from Sacramento, Fresno, and their environs. Two came directly from out of state—one from Washington, the other from Ohio. Thus Warren achieved a nice north-south balance, a matter not to be taken lightly by any California governor.

In gathering his official family, Warren again pioneered in starting a technique since copied in some other states and somewhat fitfully by his gubernatorial heirs in California. To satisfy his bent for thoroughness in finding the facts in the realm of appointment, he in later years relied partly on the same contrivance used so beneficially in other areas: citizen advisory committees to advance candidates for his scrutiny. Besides those whose lineage ran to important segments of society, these units always contained among their membership at least a sprinkling of specialists from the fields in question. This proved a real boon in attracting qualified persons into competition. Certain directors of corrections, of mental hygiene, of social welfare, and of the California youth authority were enlisted in that manner. All four were either in government ventures then in their respective callings or had been so engaged for a number of years in the past.

This device was first put to the test in 1944 in recruiting a head man for the state's new corrections department, itself a Warren creation. The Governor requested his personnel authorities to comb the entire country for someone to run the new agency. Even though it was a non–civil service position, advisory written and oral examinations were conducted. The last hurdle was an extensive interview before a special panel, also nationwide in makeup. Its participants were the current director of United States prisons; his predecessor, who was then chairman of New York's parole setup; an associate justice of the federal circuit court in Washington, D.C.; the past leader of the state League of Women Voters; and the president of the California personnel board. Suggested to Warren and welcomed by him was Richard A. McGee, a man with a lengthy background in

penal work who was then director of public institutions for
Washington State. McGee was recognized across the land as a
top authority in the field, and his seasoned ability led to his
retention by both Republican Governor Goodwin Knight and
Democratic Governor Edmund G. Brown. Brown even promoted
him to administrator of the superagency that later housed corrections, even though McGee was nominally a Republican.

Strictly professional counsel was used in choosing a new
director of mental hygiene in 1949, when Warren asked Frank J.
Tallman to come west on a recommendation from the deans of
California's five medical colleges. This gentleman had a twenty-
two-year record of administration, practice, and teaching in
medicine and psychiatry. He was Ohio's mental hygiene commissioner from 1944 to 1947.

Combined expert and lay consultation was instrumental in
Warren's 1950 hiring of a new director of social welfare. In
February he set up an eleven-man body to screen prospects and
told it to spare no effort in canvassing the country for the best.
This unit has as members the deans of the respective schools of social
work at U.S.C. and U.C.L.A., a professor in that discipline
from Berkeley, the chairman of the state welfare board, the state's
finance director, and the presiding officer of the state personnel
board, as well as delegates from the Supervisors' Association, the
Federation of Labor, the Catholic Welfare Bureau and Community
Chest in Los Angeles, and the National Broadcasting
Company. Months of painstaking exploration resulted in the
nomination of Charles I. Schottland, a Los Angeles Democrat.
His professional service dated from 1927 and he had held a
host of private and governmental posts at state, national, and
international levels since then. He had even put in a tour of
duty with the United Nations Relief and Rehabilitation Administration. Partly because he had been on General Eisenhower's
staff in World War II and primarily because of his accomplishments
for Warren, he was hired in 1954 as President Eisenhower's
commissioner of social welfare. This prototype of high-management
professionalization set by the Governor and duplicated
thereafter in the state steered national attention increasingly

toward California (a focus reinforced by her growing political potency) as a reservoir of superior administrative talent.

In 1952 Warren invited another Democrat, Heman G. Stark, to take command of the state's youth authority. Stark was appointed from a list of ten aspirants who had been examined by a five-man body composed of representatives from the Prison Association, the state bar, the Probation and Parole Officers' Association, the California Teachers' Association and—with bygones apparently bygones—the California Medical Association. Stark had been in juvenile and correctional enterprises continuously since 1928. A former officer of the Los Angeles County Probation Department, he was head of field services for the state agency at the time of his elevation.

Almost all other department directors were in some phase of government service in their respective specialties when inducted into Warren's administration or in past years. Several were on California's payroll already when named to their jobs. Most of these were highly placed and long-standing permanent administrators in the area in question. Their ascent to the top rung of the ladder was most deserving according to the Governor: "We should encourage things of this kind so that men who have served the state faithfully in civil service positions can aspire to be the heads of these big departments. . . ."[15] He even retained an Olson confidant, Democrat William J. Cecil, as his first director of agriculture. Cecil had worked for the national A.A.A. and was a state civil service assistant director when Warren's predecessor advanced him in 1941.

Several other members of Warren's official family were men high in executive ranks. Included were his first and second heads of public works, in 1943 and 1951 (the second, Frank Durkee, was a Democrat), an employment chief picked in 1947, a natural-resources director named in 1953, the fire marshal throughout his governorship, an insurance commissioner promoted in 1951, and the man recruited in 1948 to take charge of the motor-vehicles agency. The last-named, Alvin Henderson, was the first

---

[15] *Sacramento Bee*, Dec. 17, 1942, p. 2.

career officer ever to be put in command of the agency, traditionally a patronage preserve at the upper strata. He had been with the public works department since 1920 and was its civil service deputy director when transferred to motor vehicles. Replacing Cecil as agricultural director in 1944 was Anson Brock, department head under both Governors Rolph and Merriam. The grand prize in tenure went to Democrat Edwin M. Daugherty, corporations commissioner throughout the Warren administration. Daugherty could easily be counted with the career officialdom, since he had the distinction of serving no fewer than seven California chief executives since his 1921 appointment by Governor William D. Stephens and before his 1954 retirement under Governor Goodwin Knight.

California's top-level administration was enriched by those who had been ranking executives in other jurisdictions as well. Already mentioned have been corrections director McGee, who came to California from Washington following key prison posts at Leavenworth, Kentucky, and Rikers Island, New York, and tours of duty elsewhere, and in mental hygiene Ohio's Frank Tallman, who had held numerous positions earlier in New York. They were joined by such men as James Bryant, Seth Gordon, and Charles Purcell. Bryant was engaged in social welfare endeavors in several states and supervised Michigan's program in that field before joining California's employment agency and climbing its hierarchy to the apex. A Pennsylvania wildlife authority for many years, Gordon was at one time manager and, later, executive director of that state's game commission. Purcell, Warren's first public works director, served his earlier years in various engineering capacities for the state of Oregon and the federal government. He had also superintended construction of the famed San Francisco–Oakland Bay Bridge.

Several other directors were in local or national public posts in their fields when summoned by the Governor. Charles Schottland and Heman Stark had been discussed previously. The finance department, so crucial for its control and staff functions relative to the rest of the executive branch and embodying the critical task of budget preparation, was under the management of James Dean during most of Warren's governorship. Dean was the seasoned city manager of Sacramento before he transferred to the capitol. Dr. Wilton Halverson, the Governor's public health chieftain, was a former Pasadena city health officer and had held that same title for all Los Angeles County. Brigadier General Warren Hannum, United States Army Corps of Engineers and headquarters-division commandant for San Francisco, joined Warren's administration as natural-resources head in 1944. Charles Wollenberg, veteran supervisor of San Francisco's institutions, accepted Warren's 1943 bid to head California's social welfare structure. That same year Warren talked Karl Holton, Los Angeles County probation director, into taking over the state youth authority. Still other prime Warren lieutenants were individuals of no little private background. Perhaps most illustrative was Paul Scharrenberg, industrial relations director for the entirety of Warren's tenure in Sacramento. A confirmed and spirited unionist, the durable Scharrenberg was secretary of the state Federation of Labor from 1911 to 1936.

Two early additions to the Governor's administrative team came largely by way of the spoils route. However, one of them was a long-time private practitioner of his specialty and the other was, of all things, a registered Democrat. In the second instance, for the directorship of motor vehicles Warren named Gordon Garland, retiring assembly speaker and leader of the anti-Olson faction—the so-called economy bloc. Still, Warren could with some legitimacy claim nonpartisanship in that action. Long an activist in GOP politics, Herbert Scudder was real estate commissioner from 1943 to 1948. A state assemblymen from 1925 to 1940, Scudder was a former vice chairman and the incumbent secretary of the Republican state central committee when he received the gubernatorial appointment. Yet he had also been in the real estate business since 1920. Emphasizing the frequent inseparability of merit factors and considerations of favoritism was the 1951 advancement of assistant insurance commissioner John Maloney to the directorship of his department. Although he had been a civil servant all his adult life, it certainly did him no harm to be the son of venerable liberal Republican assemblyman and former state senator Thomas Maloney. The older man was one of the most faithful Warren devotees throughout these years.

The Governor's Council

Many legislative measures sponsored by the Governor were nurtured through the different layers of the civil service and refined by these primarily professional managers of the departments and agencies, in itself a form of nonpartisan sponsorship. Minor items and technical legal changes were customarily sent directly to the lawmakers without gubernatorial clearance. The more important proposals in the legislative agenda were also prepared by the executive establishment in the fall months preceding the convening of assembly and senate. However, these matters were always reviewed by Warren's legislative secretary for conformity with his policy goals. Issues of especially controversial character or points that the Governor intended to claim for himself were discussed thoroughly with him, although his "must" bills were usually phrased in the most general terminology possible. He allowed generous leeway for both administrative drafters and legislators in ultimately attaining the ends in question. A large portion of this preliminary negotiation and planning took place in a long-standing institution, one that lay in limbo before Warren's governorship—the Governor's Council.

Most American chief executives find need of some official apparatus for counsel on programmatic matters, coordination of frequently widespread and complex governmental functions, and infusion of a modicum of cooperative spirit and endeavor among their principal aides. The President's cabinet is designed ideally to fulfill these purposes. A purely informal tool, its exact constitution and utilization are dependent upon presidential whim. In the states the use of a formal advisory mechanism is even more erratic. In many states it simply does not exist. In others the governor, after the habit of some past Presidents, interprets the relevant provisions to mean informal meetings of a few administrative favorites who have his confidence. In still other states, while there may be constitutional, statutory, or customary underpinnings for such units, the membership, the frequency of sessions, and the proceedings are multifarious enough to defy categorization. However, only in a small minority of jurisdictions are all agency leaders assembled regularly to try to fulfill the aims of policy development, liaison, and unity.

California was only one of a handful of states in which such intentions were substantially met during Earl Warren's time. The Governor's Council was instituted by statute in 1927 under C. C. Young and it consists of all department directors named by the chief executive. Governor Brown relegated it to a minor role with the launching of eight new "superagencies," each one to house and control several related departments, agencies, boards, and commissions. The administrators of these bigger entities, along with certain other elected and appointed functionaries, met recurrently as a new "cabinet." Ronald Reagan has reduced the number of top administrators to three. Yet when Warren took over in 1943, the council was the sole forum, and merely on paper at that. For in spite of legal stipulations that it gather once monthly at a specific time fixed by the chief executive, it had fallen into disuse under Governors Rolph (1931–34), Merriam (1934–39), and Olson (1939–43). With his penchant for collaboration, Warren habitually mustered his colleagues on the last Monday of each month—a logical sequel to the staff conferences he regularly summoned as Alameda district attorney and later as state attorney general.

The Governor not only made the council a viable organization; he constantly pushed for a broader membership. Legislative enactments that he advocated raised its total from fifteen to twenty-three between 1943 and 1953. On his own initiative he brought other state leaders, notably the elective constitutional officers, into its fold to secure maximum unity throughout the administrative structure. His successors followed that precedent.

The Governor insisted that each council member or his designated deputy be present. Almost everyone in attendance was called upon for an oral accounting of departmental undertakings

since the last session and for any new thoughts for the future—
the majority of these being comparatively concise and unspecif-
ic. A few pressing issues were emphasized at each meeting and
those whose fields most appertained were thoroughly interrogated
by Warren and by their associates. These congregations kept each
agency head briefed on important events in domains other than
his own. They gave every man a chance to sit down with his
peers routinely for better mutual acquaintance, something designed to accomplish the goals of better over-all coordination and sense of teamwork. Here was a forum for exchange
of interdepartmental information and for ameliorating jurisdictional conflicts, for creating an attitude of group-mindedness
and identification with the administration as a whole.

More significantly, the council meetings were a valuable public relations arm for the Governor personally. The press was
always there and the general public had a standing invitation
to attend. Warren went to great lengths to pose appropriate
questions and to maneuver the conversation along lines that
reflected credit upon his stewardship in office. Furthermore, his
feel for proper timing was masterly. He turned the talk toward
educational concerns near the beginning of any school term, in
the direction of forest and conservation practices during periods
of peak fire hazard, along recreational paths at the height of the
camping and skiing seasons, to highway safety matters as major
holidays approached, and into health channels at the crest of
flu epidemics. Here again was patent his keen desire for partnership with the masses through conscientious reporting and the
hope of sowing for himself the seeds for subsequent bipartisan
backing.

Still, the plenary sessions of the council were too large and
heterogeneous to assist the Chief Executive on the spot in policymaking. Their openness to press and public, while it satisfied
some worthwhile political goals for Warren, was a distinct dis-
advantage in another way. Frank disclosures that might hint at
disagreement in the official family or raise questions regarding
its proficiency could scarcely be tolerated. The parleys had to be
restricted to discussions of fairly innocuous content. To compen-

sate for these defects, Warren instigated other practices to sound out more completely his ranking subordinates on substantive matters. He had them submit detailed written communiqués of their activities for the preceding thirty days and of any projected enterprises not later than ten days before each meeting. These documents went immediately to the departmental secretary for analysis and summary. The secretary's condensations and the originals were passed on to the Governor for his study and perusal. Warren spent many hours in consultation with his aide pouring over these materials for legislative ideas and possible lines of further inquiry at the next meeting. Copies of the original reports were forwarded to each agency head, helping them keep up to date on their colleagues' activities. The Chief Executive's assistant in this area served not only as the major link between him and his subordinates but also as council secretary, in which capacity he compiled an agenda for forthcoming conferences.

Warren also tried to draw out more crystallized and concrete ideas from his top lieutenants by creating council subcommittees, more confined entities composed of those whose duties were similar. To illustrate, an "institutions and social welfare" unit was made up of those from employment, youth and adult authorities, corrections, industrial relations, mental hygiene, public health, social welfare, and natural resources. These smaller groups convened for more candid, give-and-take bargaining with the Governor, undisturbed by the glare of publicity. Sometimes they were held a few days before the parent body was scheduled to stress their subject. They were frequently convened in the afternoon following council adjournment for more thorough follow-up.

Warren was also an inveterate conversationalist with his immediate staff of personal advisers prior to sending bills into the legislative hoppers. A fair portion of his day was spent closeted not only with the departmental liaison officer but, in particular, with his legislative secretary. The secretary was charged with putting the finishing touches on the gubernatorial program, urging its passage with the lawmakers, and keeping his superior posted on developments in the two chambers. Usually brought into the proceedings was his executive secretary, the man in over-all command of the office force and responsible for coordinating their tasks. A Democrat, William T. Sweigert, held that job throughout Warren's governorship. Aides for press relations, research, clemency and appointments, invitations and travel, and a private secretary, all with appropriate subordinates and a clerical staff divided into different sections, completed the Governor's office.

Thus Earl Warren resorted to an aggregation of sources for guidance in policy matters: legislators, interest-group representatives (individually and collectively in those rather unique citizen gatherings), and his official family of generally expert professionals in substantive fields, undergirded by a phalanx of trained civil servants and his immediate personal advisory corps. Sometimes it was possible to pinpoint the exact parentage of given proposals; more often they were a blend that came from several of the above-mentioned wellsprings. Such an amalgam in itself gave rise to a form of nonpartisan agenda for the affairs of state, reinforced by Warren's dedicated aversion to purely partisan sources for governmental programs. And his platform planks certainly encountered a high degree of bipartisan reception, both pro and con, when they were taken up by California's legislators.

CHAPTER IV

Earl Warren: Legislative Advocate

Long nurtured on the doctrine of separation of powers, many Americans find it difficult to comprehend the present immersion of executives in legislative pursuits. Nationally and in many states the administration is the moving force in lawmaking, the primary initiator and developer of proposals. A well-tested truism is "the executive proposes, the legislature disposes." To appreciate this phenomenon one must recall two factors. First is the inexorable trend toward complexity in policymaking, impelling legislators increasingly to look to the source that commands both expertise and data essential to a meaningful propagation of governmental ideas. Secondly, the pervasiveness of an expanding and proficient communications system focuses popular attention on the affairs of Presidents and governors. Maximum efficiency and coherence in nurturing public programs today demands administrative participation—often even interference—in the domain of the legislators in attempting to bridge the gap of constitutional separation.

Facts of political life in America also impel such a course, because the two branches represent contrasting and diverse constituencies. Chief executives owe fealty to mass sentiment and broad-based interests. Legislators must give their loyalty to more confined and specific pressures that differ from area to area. The assemblyman, senator, or representative is usually more dependent on such local concerns for his political existence than to anything the President or governor may say or do. Besides partisan and other differences, this fact of political life alone aggravates the legal division of authority. Differing terms of office exaggerate the dichotomy. However, the intricacies of statute preparation and passage compel the two branches to try to pull together, their built-in antagonisms notwithstanding. On their part, modern chief executives feel duty-bound to employ traditional methods and constantly search out new methods for bending lawmakers to their will. An examination of their operations in this sphere over a period of time leads to the conclusion that variation and innovation is the rule. Still, there is a recognizable core of powers and responsibilities possessed by the Presdent and by his counterparts in statehouses across the land, encompassing formal messages, summoning legislators in extraordinary session, various forms of veto, the use of patronage and pork, informal arm twisting, and reliance on mass public relations.

The Warren Theme: Legislative Independence

As California's governor, Earl Warren had at his beck and call all of these formal and extralegal prerogatives. Yet his style of dealing with the assembly and the senate departed from practices elsewhere. He was an extremist in shunning party channels, given the state's political climate and his own predelictions. While there seems to be a trend toward close, mutual involvement by the legislative and the executive in lawmaking ventures, this was decidedly less so under Warren. Quick to point out that he would defer to the legal independence of the two houses and vowing to avoid gubernatorial paternalism regarding their proceedings, he belabored a policy of "mutual respect and separate responsibility." This was the best guarantee of continued progress in solving public problems. In his opinion that posture would eliminate "blind partisanship or personal controversy,"[1] deterrents to official performance. He promised to follow that course throughout his governorship, after its frank affirmation in 1943: "I recognize you, the legislature, as a coordinate branch of democratic government, possessed of the dignity and the right to meet when you desire, and to plan and

---

[1] Radio Address, May 31, 1946, *Warren Speeches.*

initiate legislation which is just as much in keeping with the public wish as that which I may suggest. I want to restore and maintain a balance of understanding and confidence, which, through mutuality of effort, facilitates action in behalf of the people as a whole."[2]

Warren's noninterference pledge was a matter of devotion and he moved rapidly to convince the legislators of his good intentions. Shortly after he was sworn in for the first time, he called a number of lawmakers, Democrats and Republicans alike, to meetings which helped originate administration bills. He proclaimed that the morning hours would henceforth be open to conversations with assemblymen and senators and promised that throughout the years his door would never be closed to them. Apparently startled by such deference from the executive and wary of entering the premises unescorted (having been cowed by Culbert Olson), many individual solons at first refused to venture into the lair. Emboldened by company, they soon began showing up in small groups. Sometimes entire standing committees dropped by to assist in preparing possible lines of statutory action.

Warren continually cautioned department heads against "lobbying." There was to be no "pressure" applied to lawmakers by gubernatorial subordinates. The subordinates were expected to present data crucial to administration measures and to argue loyally and diligently for their passage, but only at open and regularly scheduled hearings, not in secretive encounters. There was an earnest attempt by Warren's underlings to conform to these injunctions, although the temptation was apparently intense enough on occasion to cause their violation.

Warren flatly declined to meddle in selections of legislative officers, even when his individual popularity and political power were at their highest, after his double-nomination victory in 1946. At the beginning of 1947 the door was left ajar for such maneuvering in the assembly. Speaker Charles W. Lyon had left the scene to challenge Judge Goodwin Knight in the 1946 GOP

---

[2] *Inaugural Address of January 4, 1943* (Sacramento: 1943), p. 5.

primary for lieutenant governor (he lost the race). In a bow to
partisanship, tradition has it, the speakership goes to the majority
party. The Chief Executive's sympathies, while hard to pinpoint
because of his reticence on internal legislative operations, lay
either with Glendale's C. Don Field or Alfred Wollenberg of
San Francisco, author of his 1945 compulsory health insurance
proposal. Most decidedly Warren's affection did not belong to the
third Republican contender, Sam Collins of Orange County.
Collins' political philosophy paralleled that of Calvin Coolidge
and he was the entry of liquor lobbyist Artie Samish. Wollenberg
quickly withdrew and gave his support to Feld, but to no avail.
Collins won handily. If Warren was chagrined at the outcome, he
failed to show it. He said simply that "the people are entitled
to independent government. I believe they voted for that kind of
government in this state at the last election."[3]

A number of specifics pertaining to the tenor of California
politics and to Warren's independent demeanor can be offered in
further explanation of his legislative relations. First, he was as
a matter of conviction a constitutional fundamentalist (a fact
that may come as a shock to some of his detractors today) in
respecting the widest possible separation of legislative, executive,
and judicial provinces. Furthermore, the decrepitude of California's political parties and the character of her electoral laws
injected an individualism into the minds of assemblymen and
senators the same as it did into the minds of executives. His
own biases notwithstanding, the Governor felt that a stronger
hand with the lawmakers would be futile. A closely related influence on gubernatorial behavior here was the Olson lesson.
Warren was an astute and observant student. His predecessor's
frustrations and the tumultuous and cantankerous atmosphere
which enveloped the two branches at that time would probably
have alone been sufficient to shock Warren into a cooperative
stance, other motivations aside.

In still another manner state politics shaped the Governor's
contacts with the solons. The assembly speaker and the senate

---

[3] *Sacramento Bee,* Nov. 27, 1946, p. 4.

rules committee make all committee appointments, including chairmen. This they ordinarily do without the approval of the chief executive, although he is permitted to suggest who should head the lower-house ways and means unit that appropriates money for the budget. It was not surprising, then, that many committees were weighted heavily with persons whose views were not in agreement with Warren's. To apply force in any significant degree could have turned their natural coolness into indignant hostility.

Contrary to many other jurisdictions, including the national, committee structure in California's two legislative chambers is regulated neither by partisanship nor by strict seniority. Some have a majority, or a chairman, or both, from the minority party. Several committees in each chamber bore a definitely conservative Republican stamp at different sessions during Warren's administration and looked with sullen mien upon his governorship. In other instances Democrats dominated given units, although they remained the minority in the legislature as a whole throughout those years. While the Democrats may often have appreciated many gubernatorial propositions, the compulsion to play the loyal opposition sometimes provoked them into obstinance.

Constitutionalist, realist, student—Warren was all of these. He was also a moralist of sorts, for he acted as he did partly out of fear of being trapped into "shady deals." He refused to trade his signature on lawmakers' pet projects for passage of items he was advocating at the time. In short, he was not much of a logroller, nor was he prone to use either threat of the veto or what little patronage he had at his command.

Legislative Leadership, Warren Style

Warren called attention to different California issues that should be met through statutory action in his messages at the commencement of each legislative session. He set up goals and suggested avenues that might be followed by assemblymen and senators in attaining them. His recommendations were ordinarily broad in expression, phrased to antagonize as few as possible and to permit the members great leeway in reaching final conclusions. In 1951 he commented upon industrial accident and jobless insurance in these words: "The sense of security that enables men and women who work for wages to do their best, will also be enhanced if they know that adequate provision has been made for them under the workmen's compensation and unemployment insurance programs. I urge you to examine these systems to determine whether they are fully serving the humanitarian purposes for which they were established."[4]

The Chief Executive was primarily concerned with finding some solutions to outstanding problems. If these could not be achieved through his own programs, then at least they should be effected through some other appropriate plans. Naturally he tended to favor certain measures. Still, it was not characteristic of him to insist upon passage of a specific bill as the sole means of securing a given end. Rarely dogmatic regarding particulars, not dissatisfied if the legislature failed to pay him total homage, he was ready to accept alternatives if they led essentially to the same results. This pliability and resiliency, added to his independent outlook, caused some, including 1946 foe Robert Kenny, to call the Governor a poor legislative leader. Nevertheless, contrary opinion seems to predominate. Even the Democratic floor leader in the assembly during much of Warren's administration praised Warren's deftness of approach.[5] Warren's style of "direction" was quite productive, approximately 90 percent of his suggestions becoming law.

Although governors across the country have generally experienced success whatever their method of legislative relations, few had as good fortune as did California's governor. Yet quantitative appraisals can be misleading, overemphasizing number and excluding quality and importance of bills. Several key Warren measures failed the test of assembly or senate scrutiny, and some of these might have fared better had the Governor put more pressure on the lawmakers. While the judgment is

---

[4] *Inaugural Address of January 8, 1951* (Sacramento: 1951), p. 8.
[5] Hon. Julian Beck. Interview, May 11, 1956.

subjective, perhaps compulsory health insurance and civil rights
are exemplary. However, a moderating thought from his former
executive secretary intrudes here—in California's political milieu
"no man can take the lead in better manner than to tell openly
and positively what should be done on state problems."[6]

Harold Levering of Los Angeles, GOP assemblyman of the
stand-pat wing during Warren's tenure, told me that the Governor's "fancied independence" of the legislature was mere "lip
service." The Chief Executive was shrewed enough to "put the
screws on those few in his clique that he could," claimed Levering.[7] However, authority has it that the Governor resisted the
allurement of "strong techniques" of legislative manipulation.
He was distinctly averse to such favorite Olsonisms as strongly
worded demands for action by the two houses, occasionally
summoning legislators to his desk for a stern lecture, belaboring
the solons' unwillingness to completely accept his terms, threaten-
ing to send them back to private life at the ensuing election, or
overtly brandishing the veto.

There was another good reason for Warren's rare invocation
of the veto or even a hint of it. When one phrases statutory ideas
in generalities, leaving specifics to be hammered out in the legislature, he places himself in the situation of having to accept the
final product. However, there is little reason to doubt that
Warren did somtimes imply a possible use of the veto sanction,
that his allusions to steps that should be taken in legislative
circles were on many occasions potent influences in the ultimate
conclusions reached. Nevertheless, no ranking administrator, regardless of his own biases or the setting in which he must function, can remain entirely aloof from legislative proceedings.
Warren was no exception. To guide the assemblymen and the
senators toward certain ends, he relied heavily upon two informal
tactics—personal appeal and mass public relations.

---

[6] Hon. William T. Sweigert (D), U.S. district court judge, former
judge of the Superior Court of San Francisco County, former executive
secretary to Gov. Warren and former deputy to Atty. Gen. Warren. Interview, Jan. 20, 1957.

[7] Interview, Feb. 14, 1957.

As he did in initiating measures, Warren made beneficial use
of meetings with individuals and small groups of lawmakers.
Ranging from solemn confabs to relaxed chats, they were another
move in the direction of unity in resolving public issues. These
discussions were carried on by the Governor with a disposition
toward compromise of divergent viewpoints, and the sentiments
of those who disagreed with him were given courteous consideration, if not always acceptance. Here was an effort by the Chief
Executive to create a friendly, personal relationship between
himself and as many lawmakers as possible in both parties. If this
could be done, the more emphatic forms of urging would not
be necessary. He preferred to approach the members as reasonable, intelligent persons who were aware of the difficulties confronting California and of the need for their amelioration.

Furthermore, there was no fixed, enduring body of Warren
supporters within each chamber. The legal authorship of propositions embodying his recommendations varied by topic and by
party. For example, Democrat John F. Shelly (later San Francisco mayor) bore the main responsibility for senate sponsorship
of the Governor's 1946 call for disability payments under unemployment compensation. While given assemblymen and
senators usually voted with him on the floor or in committee,
this was not true in every instance. There was no clique of
intimates with whom Warren counseled and upon whom he
depended at each session. To quote former legislative secretary
Beach Vasey: "We had to play with a different team each day."[8]

Warren had an irresistible preference for "open politics" and
thus a virtual obsession with public relations. Time and again
he used the stratagem of going to the people to try to construct
massive bipartisan sympathy for his measures and himself. He
hoped thereby to remove any obstacles in the path of his projects
thrown up in the legislature. The famed citizen advisory groups
discussed in the previous chapter were, among other things,
forums for arousing popular approval for administration objectives. Those of continuing duration could always be counted on
to back the Governor on many points during subsequent meet-

---

[8] Interview, May 3, 1956.

ings of the lawmakers. No chief executive in earlier California history appreciated the potentialities of the communications media as fully as did Warren. He invited newspaper reporters to any assemblage of note. They were ubiquitous at citizen bodies, many conclaves with legislators, monthly convocations of the official family, and other parleys, both substantive and ceremonial. While the twice-weekly press conferences held throughout his governorship were by no means as recurrent as in some other states, there was little need for more regular confabs; journalists were presented many other opportunities by Warren.

Probably the best illustration of Warren's activity in this connection was the radio "Report to the People" (when television was in its infancy). Put into operation but sparingly during his first term, these statewide broadcasts were generally transmitted once monthly during the last seven years of his residency in Sacramento. They were sometimes used more frequently during sessions of the assembly and the senate. Each broadcast was ordinarily confined to a single substantive question, usually in interview format. This was not only an auspicious occasion for broad publicity but a chance to offset the blandishments of interest groups upon the solons, contagious entreaties in a state lacking aggressive parties. Warren candidly acknowledged the validity of that tactic. The progress of his agenda, and any setbacks to portions of it received at legislative or lobbying hands, came in for a thorough airing at the proper time.

In 1945 the Governor was frank and specific in resisting moves for higher taxes: "I am opposed to this program. First, because increased revenue is not necessary to finance state government. Secondly, because people are already carrying an excessively heavy tax load. Third, because federal taxes are pyramiding to pay for the war, it is the duty of state government to hold its taxes down. And fourth, raising of unnecessary tax monies encourages new spending habits in government, and piles an additional financial load on the backs of the people."[9] Partly because of his plea, rates held firm that year.

One of Warren's more elaborate exhortations occurred in 1947.

---

[9] Radio Address, Mar. 10, 1945, *Warren Speeches.*

The subject was a possible expansion of highway construction through augmented gasoline and oil assessments, a fruitful field for strained group and sectional relations in the state ever since. Asked the obviously leading question as to whether the legislature realized the seriousness of the situation, he answered: "Yes, it does. From the very beginning the overwhelming majority of the state senate has been wholeheartedly in favor of the program, but, unfortunately, the assembly has so far been five or six votes short of the majority required. . . . I refuse to believe that with people dying on our congested highways as they are today, the legislature will go home from this session without taking proper steps to end the slaughter. . . ."[10] These were strong words, words that preceded a denunciation of the "oil lobby" that was holding up his measure. It took little time for the bill to clear both chambers. California's immense and expensive highway building boom had begun.

Perhaps the Chief Executive reached the height of anger in 1949. At that time he roundly castigated the lawmakers' lethargy and pressure machinations pertaining to his request for hospitalization payments under disability compensation. He commented testily that "the California Medical Association, the insurance lobby, and powerful employer groups moved into legislative circles and blocked the entire suggestion. Just keep in mind that every cent of the money involved in this program is collected from employees, and that the employers' groups are not out a thin dime for the program. Then try to justify what has happened if you can." Warming as he went along, Warren charged that "the California Medical Association rose in its dignity to announce that such a plan was an entering wedge for health insurance. Insurance groups marched in and protested that such an idea would disturb the amount of service they must render under California law. Employer groups waved their arms in general opposition. . . ." Now he offered this challenge: "I am still waiting to find the legislator or lobbyist who can explain this situation in terms of economy, efficiency, or fairness.

[10] Public Service Broadcast, June 2, 1947, *Warren Speeches.*

I still want to know why it is not economy to give the worker more for his tax dollar and, in particular, I want to know why the worker should be denied the use of his own money for a hospital bill when he is in dire need. . . ." Winding up with a burst of oratory perhaps more revealing of his methodology and motives than any other, he told his audience pointedly: "I want the workers of the state to know this situation and I hope they will watch the California legislature during the next month to see just what happens when powerful lobby groups gang up and try to impose their will on the people."[11]

The Governor's occasional dissatisfaction with the assembly-men and senators was not confined to particulars. Anticipating that his days as chief executive would end without his securing certain key items, feeling that what would probably be his last regular session had not adjourned on a generally productive note, and undoubtedly suffering the wear and tear of more than ten years of dickering with the two houses, he expressed general displeasure with the outcome of their 1953 deliberations: "The legislature's attitude . . . seemed to reflect a determination to by-pass everything that might involve change or expansion. Outside of the highway bill, there was little of major importance. Many important bills were proposed, many legislators fought valiantly for badly needed measures. But the prevailing do-nothing pressures were too strong for them. . . . It was a session devoted largely to trying to stand still."[12]

On the whole, Warren praised legislative ventures more than he defamed them. He was quick to commend those who had allied with him and to give thanks for whatever advances were made. With the understandable exaltation of a highly successful freshman, he was unhesitating in the compliments he lavished in 1943: "The legislature worked efficiently, avoided petty par-tisanship, and wasteful bickering. It stuck to its job, kept the war uppermost in its mind, and after a constructive session, adjourned earlier than any session in the past thirty-six years. My relations with it were cordial. We discussed problems frankly

11 Public Service Broadcast, June 7, 1949, *Warren Speeches.*
12 Public Service Broadcast, June 16, 1953, *Warren Speeches.*

and almost without exception arrived at a satisfactory conclusion. . . ."[13] His eulogy to the 1946 special meeting was one that well displayed his patience and dedication to moderate progress: "A great majority of the things I recommended went through, and I can derive a great deal of satisfaction from the things that were accomplished. There were, of course, a few things that didn't get through and one or two with which I didn't agree did get through—but I take the view that it is better to be grateful for what was accomplished than to be resentful over what wasn't accomplished. We can always keep on trying for those things we believe in but didn't get."[14] The last, incidentally, was something he could not do in 1953.

Warren was quite conscious of his popularity with the electorate, probably the most meaningful ingredient in his legislative influence. California did have an individualistic political environment that resulted in many split tickets. Still, the coattail effect could not be utterly ignored by candidates for lesser posts in California. True, the Governor was not a party stalwart who delighted in heading slates of GOP ballot hopefuls. Nor was he given to the game of electoral expulsion of those who had annoyed him. Yet in his unobstrusive manner he wanted his adversaries in both parties to understand that they could be tabbed anti-Warren. As such, they would not be entitled to reap whatever political rewards might be forthcoming from a pro-Warren stand.

One can turn again to Warren's debate with Kenny on the subject of legislative relations in the 1946 statehouse race to summarize the posture he took with the assembly and senate. In reply to the criticism of his rival, he remarked: "You will find from the record that I have established and maintained a policy of open dealing with the legislature. . . . There has been no trading, no coercion, no surrender of prerogatives in dealings between executive and legislature. I have dealt with the legis-

---

[13] Address to the Commonwealth Club of California, San Francisco, Jan. 7, 1944, *Warren Speeches.*

[14] Radio Talk, Mar. 30, 1946, *Warren Speeches.*

lature in open message and in open conference . . . and it has paid to the extent of accomplishing ninety percent of those things I recommended. . . . That I asked for more, and did not get it, is something for which I hold no resentment. This is one of the inevitable results of our American system of divided responsibility—a system that is our only bulwark against the greater evil of government by one man, or by one faction, or by a machine."[15]

California's Legislature: The Debasement of Partisanship

Given the state's political envoronment, California's legislature has long been less partisan in both organization and voting than most legislatures. More significant have been factional or interest coalition, or regional schisms that often cut mercilessly through the parties. The Warren epoch was the most nonpartisan in the internal functioning of the state's two legislative houses, a situation that greatly pleased the Governor and one for which he shared some responsibility. More than elsewhere the assembly speaker in California wins his position because of his careful cultivation of a personal, bipartisan following and its allied groups, although he is a member of the majority party. These factors are even more pronounced in relation to the upper chamber's president pro tempore and the rules committee that he heads.

The 1947 speakership contest won by Sam Collins of Orange County has been mentioned previously. He openly wooed Democrats in his successful bid and the GOP was virtually split down the middle. In fact, only 46 percent of Collins' entourage consisted of his fellow Republicans. Fifty-four percent of the Democrats, though less in numbers, rallied to his cause.[16] True

---

[15] Address to San Francisco Campaign Luncheon, Apr. 24, 1946, *Warren Speeches*.

[16] William Buchanan, *Legislative Partisanship: The Deviant Case of California* (Berkeley: Univ. of California Press, 1963), p. 29, Fig. 2.

to the code, the assembly's new leader saw that the Democrats were able to exchange their credits for important committee posts. Through most of Collins' tenure a bipartisan clique was turned into an interlocking directorate that overlapped no fewer than four crucial committees: (1) public morals, which regulated the liquor industry and horse racing, (2) manufacturing, oil, and mining industry, (3) constitutional amendments, and (4) rules, which oversees much of the management of the lower chamber. There were enough seats on these bodies for a total of thirty-seven people. Yet a plurality on each came from the same nine men, four of whom were Democrats. Collins did conform to custom and permit Warren to recommend as head of the ways and means unit Alfred Wollenberg of San Francisco, sponsor of the gubernatorial health insurance proposal and one of Collins' recent adversaries for the right to wield the gavel. However, the new speaker was still able to delay portions of the administration's program by placing men antagonistic to Warren in critical positions elsewhere. Perhaps most exemplary was the naming of Republican Jonathan Hollibaugh, Los Angeles conservative, to chair the revenue and taxation committee that raises the money for the executive budget.

Bipartisan antagonism to the Collins' "establishment" grew over the next four years and resulted in a fierce fight in 1951 over reform of the assembly rules committee. The anti-Collins forces christened themselves the "good government coalition." With the presiding officer's departure in 1953, the last of Warren's governorship, they captured the speakership for James M. Silliman of Salinas. Once in office, Silliman wasted little time in deposing committee heads and members from both parties. Chairman Hollibaugh was purged from revenue and taxation, a move that pleased Warren. Nevertheless, the new protectorate was by no means uniformly pro-Warren or under Warren's control. This was readily illustrated by the Speaker's choice of Harold Levering, GOP tory from Los Angeles, for majority floor leader.

The purely partisan machinery has been left largely unoiled over the years in California's legislature, particularly in the senate. This is perhaps most manifest in the case of the floor leaders. He who speaks technically for the majority in the assembly has long been anointed by the speaker and is in reality more the latter's alter ego than a true chief of a partisan camp. In neither the majority nor the minority floor position is aggressive partisan direction the usual practice, a circumstance quite strange to their counterparts in our nation's capital and in some other states. Neither have these officials ordinarily acted as the governor's spokesmen through the bond of party. Illustrative was Speaker Collins' designation of Randall Dickey as floor leader in 1947 and his succession by Harold Levering in 1953 through fiat of Speaker Silliman. Both were militant conservatives known for their lack of fondness for Earl Warren. It seemed that resistance to the Governor was part and parcel of that post during Warren's administration.

Assistant leaders or whips were unknown in California's legislature at the time of Warren's departure for the United States Supreme Court, although they now function in the lower house. While he bears credentials from the partisan group in power, the senate's president pro tempore is more field marshal to the entire chamber than partisan advocate. A minority leader is there to remind him that at least a token confrontation of the two parties should occur. Furthermore, the caucuses were not generally active during most of Warren's incumbency. Those in the assembly began to stir in the late forties and they are much more vibrant today than they were at that time. Senate caucuses were virtually moribund during the Warren years, a situation that is scarcely different now. Punishment for not following the party line (what there is of it) in either house was and still is a comparative rarity.

Given these facts, it is not surprising that party discipline has freely broken down on roll calls in California's legislature. In Congress the proportion of tallies in which the majority of the membership of each party is found on opposing sides of a question may range up to 50 percent, although ordinarily it is not that high. One assessment finds that in the lower chambers of some northeastern states those statistics vary from 60 to 90 percent. Ohio, Illinois, Kentucky, and Missouri have shown pro-

portions from 36 to 54 percent, comparable to the percentage
on Capitol Hill. Colorado's recent average was 38 percent and
Washington state's 51 percent.[17] By contrast, California's figures
during Warren's administration were the lowest, being 31 percent in 1949 and 36 percent in 1951.[18] Moreover, internal cohesion
within each party was ordinarily quite low in both houses.

One characteristic that substantially abates partisan influences
in California's legislative process is the "automatic calendar."
This augments the potency of each author in advancing his own
set of measures. California legislators have long felt more free
than the legislators of many other states to collect statutory ideas
from other sources than the strictly partisan—from constituents,
lobbies, administrative departments, and their own personal resources. Then, unless the sponsor otherwise indicates, bills are
taken up in the order in which they arrive at each phase of the
legislative operation: at the presiding officer's desk (where his
power of reference is soldom arbitrary, more often routine), in
committee, and on the floor. None of these power points were
regulated during the Warren era for purposes of partisan pro-
gramming. Thus each solon, Democrat or Republican, had then,
and still has, more opportunity than in other jurisdictions to
champion his own platform, a habitual undertaking fully sup-
ported by popular expectation.

It was partly because of such methods of procedure that Earl
Warren put forth his legislative thoughts in the imprecise
manner described. Any number of the many personal items
flooding the chambers might secure the ends he desired. Furthermore, given such a preoccupation with politically crucial individual platforms, he believed that the best policy often was
not to upset the status quo forcefully but simply to choose from
the multitude of offerings already there. A detailed agenda from
the gubernatorial office might have been pushed aside in the
competition, with rather dire political consequences. It was
better to speak in broad generalities and entrust the particulars

---

[17] See Malcolm Jewell, *The State Legislature: Politics and Practice*
(New York: Random House, 1962), pp. 51-53, and the sources he cites.

[18] Buchanan, *op cit.*, pp. 111, 127.

to those otherwise concerned with each substantive area. Those so concerned might be assemblymen and senators from either party who had the best chance of steering a bill through the current atmosphere of faction and pressure. The amorphous and highly unpredictable nature of the alliances in each California chamber further encouraged the Governor to generalize. It was too difficult to assess completely the fate of a given proposal in so inscrutable a situation. The lack of any well-disciplined partisan minority enabled Warren to be the more inexact, since he never faced a concerted, well-programmed opposition.

The Legislature Disposes: The Pattern of Action on the Warren Programs

In tracing legislative action on Warren's ideas, with special emphasis on partisan considerations, several complications are evident. His broad language meant that many points in his messages lacked the sufficient definition necessary to determine which bills he favored. Another complication is present in California as well as many other states, namely, that assembly and senate records are unrevealing (a real understatement in the case of California during the Warren period). Floor and committee discussions are not ordinarily transcribed, as they are in our national Congress. In fact, even the identity of those who cast ayes and nays is formally secret in the committees of each house. Voting details are usually given in plenary session. However, a large portion of these are on final passage of items and manifest complete or near unanimity, a clue that the decisive action on a prospective statute was in the past and forever unlisted. The determinative step taken on many gubernatorial requests was hidden in that fashion. In addition, much of Warren's agenda that was not accepted was turned down in committee, the operations of which are very obscured, with the exception of a few private documents.

Nonetheless, numerous roll calls are available on propositions openly favored or rejected by the Chief Executive, and on others of which his approval or dislike could be logically deduced from prior statements. Those do not show complete legislative results on his recommendations; yet they do give a more than adequate sampling of the tenor of backing and opposition he received from different categories of lawmakers. Some recorded votes are on the final passage of measures and others on parliamentary motions salient to them. The statistics in the chambers were obtained by me from the official journals of both assembly and senate for all regular and extraordinary meetings during Warren's administration. Procedure was traced on all bills that could reasonably be designed to achieve each goal of the Governor, as indicated in each of his communications to the solons. Of those roll calls where there was some division, assembly computations with less than ten and senate computations with only five or fewer members on one side of any question were automatically disregarded. Many others were discarded as redundant because identical or virtually the same conclusions were reached in other soundings on the same issue.

Votes picked for illustration fell into distinct categories. Two were on health, both calling for compulsory medical insurance. Eight pieces of welfare legislation sought to increase the state portion of contributions to the elderly, raise the permissible maximum of real-property qualification for old age pensions, retain assistance for child care centers, and aid those permanently and totally disabled. Twelve calculations on labor matters furnish an expression of legislative thought on possible extension of unemployment compensation to new classes of workers, a longer duration of payments to those idled, unemployment relief, machinery to help attain more job opportunities, wider coverage under the industrial-accident system, a fair employment practices commission, hospitalization stipends under disability benefits, and a postwar construction and employment fund. These twenty-two health, welfare, and labor bills are grouped here as "social" topics.

Another twenty-two roll calls are bracketed as "administrative" matters for our purposes and pertained to the subjects of taxation, government organization, and lobbying. Seven fiscal measures concerned reductions in personal income, bank and corporation franchise, and corporate income levies, as well as increments in fuel and alcoholic-beverage revenues. Another dozen were on invitations to reconstitute California's public health and social welfare setups, to create a new corrections agency, office of planning director, water pollution control board, department of water resources, and department of highway patrol, and to have Sacramento take from the counties all management of social welfare. Three others asked for stricter regulation of legislative advocates.

Calculation is made of percentages of support given the Warren position on these different bills by various classes of legislators in each chamber. The first major breakdown is by party. Here the relative degree of agreement with the Governor by Democrats and Republicans, respectively, is noted; then the number of "party votes" cast is related to the gubernatorial measures. These are tabulations where a majority of the GOP members who expressed their sentiments was pitted against over 50 percent of the Democrats who answered the roll.

A second analysis compares the stand taken by assemblymen and senators from the three biggest metropolitan centers of Los Angeles, San Francisco, and San Diego with those from all other localities in the state, defined as nonmetropolitan. This is an arbitrary allocation but one that I believe to be more meaningful than standard classifications. California was overwhelmingly urban and metropolitan throughout the Warren period (a situation even more true today). While many areas labeled nonmetropolitan here are the opposite by legal definition, they lack the variety and intensity of socio-economic problems confronting the three places with the greatest number of inhabitants. Indeed, certain California cities are more realistically rural in terms of makeup and environs, such as some in the agricultural central valley. A third division is the north-south. Here is presented the proportionate help given the Chief Executive by solons from these two large regions.

Lawmakers who responded yes were in sympathy with the Governor in most instances, although a negative sign mirrored

Warren's attitude in some cases. To compute the respective ratios of assistance he obtained, all legislators in the category under examination who participated in the decision were first added up. This total was then divided into the number of those in agreement with Warren on the question and a comparison made with other relevant groups. If no assemblymen or senators of a particular description voted on an item, no contrast is made of their percentage with that of others, since their viewpoint was completely without representation.

Scrutiny of the records for the whole of Warren's administration leads initially to a few sweeping impressions as to the assistance he secured in the legislature. His greatest over-all triumph came during the first honeymoon session in 1943, during the unity years of World War II. Nearly his entire platform became a part of the legal codes at that time. Opposition to the Governor's convictions tended to grow as his tenure in office lengthened, something experienced by many American chief executives. The years 1949 and 1953 were the most disappointing. He fared about equally well in the two houses. Yet the number of setbacks, many on critical social proposals, was somewhat larger in the assembly than in the senate, a situation that might come as a surprise to some observers. Typically, most of the Warren agenda which was rejected was buried in committee and principally in the body of origin.

Turning to statistical findings, the following pages contain a résumé of the Governor's backing from different classes of legislators in each chamber. Figures in the ensuing tables represent the *number of issues* on which the group of lawmakers named had higher percentages of alignment with Warren than the group with which it is compared. In the assembly there are thirty computations, fifteen on social and fifteen on administrative issues. In the senate fourteen votes are recapitulated, seven apiece under the two primary headings.

Most significantly, Democrats sustained the Governor more substantially than did Republicans on a slight plurality of all bills scanned for both houses, as shown in Table 4. However, there is a pronounced partisan gulf between the two basic

Table 4

SUPPORT (FLOOR VOTE) FOR WARREN POSITIONS IN CALIFORNIA LEGISLATURE:
DEMOCRATIC VS. REPUBLICAN

| | Assembly | | Senate | | |
	Dem.	Rep.	Dem.	Rep.	Tie
Social Issues	14	1	5	1	1
Nonsocial Issues	2	13	2	5	
Total	16	14	7	6	1

subject-matter categories. Democrats more firmly aligned themselves with Warren on many more social measures; much heavier Republican support obtained in the administrative field. Fourteen party votes occurred on the twenty-two social proposals, eleven in the assembly and three in the senate. Democrats joined Warren with more solidarity on *all of these,* and their sympathy for him was more pronounced on most of the remainder. Further probing uncovers a determined Democratic unity with Warren on several very crucial social propositions. On the contrary there were almost no party votes involving heavier shares of GOP aid for the Governor and the items were fewer on which they gave him more preponderant support.

Table 5 indicates that nonmetropolitan assemblymen put

Table 5

SUPPORT (FLOOR VOTE) FOR WARREN POSITIONS IN CALIFORNIA LEGISLATURE:
METROPOLITAN VS. NONMETROPOLITAN

| | Assembly | | Senate | | |
	Metrop.	Non-Metrop.	Metrop.	Non-Metrop.	Tie
Social Issues	12	3	4	2	1
Nonsocial Issues	1	14	3	4	
Total	13	17	7	6	1

forth a little more effort for Warren than metropolitan. Nevertheless, their edge did not come on social issues, for their metropolitan associates led the way on most of those questions. The reverse was true in the upper house. Senators from the three population centers were more firmly with the Governor on more points, owing here, as in the assembly, to their proportionately higher allegiance on a greater number of social measures. Table 6 underscores the much greater amity for Warren's beliefs from northerners on both classes of subject in each chamber.

Table 6

SUPPORT (FLOOR VOTE) FOR WARREN POSITIONS IN CALIFORNIA LEGISLATURE:
NORTHERN VS. SOUTHERN

| | Assembly | | | Senate | |
	North	South	Tie	North	South
Social Issues	10	5		4	3
Nonsocial Issues	11	3	1	4	3
Total	21	8	1	8	6

The most significant fact to emerge from the foregoing account is the magnitude of Democratic reinforcement for the Governor's programs in California's legislature—aid and comfort quite pronounced on most of his key ideas. Perhaps it can be put in bolder perspective by investigating further some of his cardinal legislative ideas and achievements.

PART THREE

The Warren Political Style and Public Policy: Health, Welfare, and Labor Issues

CHAPTER V

Earl Warren: Program Innovator

That Earl Warren was an advocate of cooperative endeavor, that he was a pragmatic problem solver, a progressive, and that he was an independent political operative were all shown in his espousal of various programs, particularly those in health, welfare, and labor. Certainly the epithets *builder* and *innovator* are apt descriptions of the Governor, considering his accomplishments. Probably no single state chief executive in previous American history had overseen the building of so many highways, schools, hospitals, correctional institutions, homes, or water, power, and recreational projects. Most states have never possessed, let alone erected, as many facilities as California constructed from 1943 to 1953, a pace which has accelerated greatly since that time. This prodigious output was accompanied by a number of new physical and programmatic departures.

The Governor and the Health Issue

In health ventures the Governor not only scored high on sheer attainment but exposed prime features of his political personality. He reorganized the state public health department, improved and expanded crippled-children's services, extended basic health services to cover the entire state, and built a number of new public hospitals. His talents as an innovator were particualrly evident in his early attempts to deal with what had long been a pathetic predicament of great magnitude in California and nationwide—proper provision for the mentally ill and deficient, a field that produced no little political controversy during the first few months of the Reagan governorship. In his own words the Chief Executive sought "to take California out of the asylum age and put her into the hospital age."[1] The need for accelerated public action was clear from the time he stepped into the state's top office. Overcrowding, poor treatment programs, physical deterioration, and personnel shortages were hallmarks of the mental institutions. Signaling the attack in early 1945 with a comprehensive ten-year master plan, his administration inaugurated a new department of mental hygiene, secured appropriations exceeding $134,000,000 to complete one new institution, launch two others, commence a statewide system of community clinics, enrich treatment techniques, and triple the staff. By the time Warren left office the degree of excess population at facilities for the mentally ill had actually been reduced from 1943 despite a huge increase in inmates; that same ratio for the retarded had gone up by only 4.2 percent notwithstanding a 45 percent gain in residents; the ratio of personnel to patients had climbed dramatically; and the proportion of mentally ill discharged as cured or improved rose substantially. While rapidly growing California still had shortcomings in each of these areas, even pronounced deficiencies in some, considerable progress had been made between 1943 and 1953 in moving away from the "asylum age."

Perhaps the highlight of Warren's endeavors in the mental health field was his championship of a network of outpatient clinics, a subject that underscored features of his political behavior and a lively topic under the economy-minded Reagan administration. In 1945 Warren told the lawmakers that "humanitarianism and economy link themselves as a reason for action by state government. We should have clinics . . . where people undergoing . . . strain can be treated and prevented, whenever possible, from mental crackups which will add to our hospital responsibility. . . ."[2] He requested four units in addition to the existing Langley Porter establishment in San Francisco, erected by his Democratic predecessor and today operating along with

---

[1] Public Service Address, Jan. 10, 1950, *Warren Speeches.*
[2] *Biennial Message of January 8, 1945* (Sacramento: 1945), p. 10.

the facility at U.C.L.A. as a combination clinic and neuropsychiatric training and research institute. Yet his bid was rejected by the assembly ways and means committee, dominated then by a 17 to 8 GOP margin, although one dispensary was subsequently allotted to Los Angeles. Undaunted, the Chief Executive asked the 1947 legislature for such units in Fresno, Sacramento, and San Diego, and for a second one in Los Angeles.

Many California governors have encountered the fiscal cleaver of the legislative analyst (labeled auditor in Warren's day), charged specifically with scrutinizing the gubernatorial budget to suggest cuts. It is sometimes questioned whether he and his assistants are motivated purely by monetary considerations or by broader policy concerns. It was often at the insistence of Auditor Rolland A. Vandegrift, undeniably an expert in fiscal matters but a Republican of conservative political inclinations, that Warren's fund-raising ventures frequently fell short of anticipation. Exemplary was Vandegrift's analysis for the fiscal year of 1948, when he recommended paring thirty new positions for physicians from a gubernatorial request for 714 staff additions to homes and hospitals. He alleged that "so long as the bulk of patients in our institutions are custodial cases and not subject to recovery, the real problem is one of custodial care"[3]—a conviction in direct opposition to the concepts basic to the administration's efforts. Vandergrift was apparently enchanted with the idea of confinement. For in 1947 he also said that until the clinic program proved its worth with more evidence than was then available, the assembly and the senate should deny the Chief Executive's overtures to build more units.

Warren's defense, at least in the press, fell to Carl Applegate. The deputy director of mental hygiene argued that this was no novelty but something already in being in several states and as necessary as tuberculosis, baby, or dental clinics. He observed that "it has long been recognized that if potential . . . patients can be seen in their childhood or in the early stages of their . . . disease, there is far better opportunity of preventing . . . break-

---

[3] California Legislature, *Appendix to Journal of Senate,* 57th Sess., 1947 I (Sacramento: 1947), pp. 449-50.

down or in treating the person who is already a mental case. After a person has become a long standing . . . case, it is doubly difficult to effect any permanent betterment or cure. To provide early treatment is far cheaper than to provide permanent custodial care . . . in later years."[4] Additionally, there would be incalculable savings to the community through reduction of unemployment, alcoholism, suicide, and crime. Reacting to these comments, to national publicity on the issue, and to the Governor's urging, the legislators appropriated money to construct three more facilities in Fresno, Sacramento, and San Diego and to double the staff at the Los Angeles clinic. Burgeoning enrollments at these places led to creation of others, for a total of eight during Warren's tenure.

Warren's ideas in the provinces of public and mental health were reasonably well received in the legislature. Yet in 1945 he was to sponsor for the first time another proposition with a decidedly higher potential for provoking antagonism from many lawmakers, to say nothing of most of the medical profession. It touched off an imbroglio that the Governor was to lose in the legislative arena and whose ramifications were to spread to the national scene. This was his controversial proposal for compulsory health insurance, a subject dear to his heart. This issue, probably more than any other, classified Warren as a Republican maverick and lured many Democrats in the assembly, senate, and electorate to his banner.

Certainly the Chief Executive was not plowing virgin soil, for the health insurance question had been discussed and debated for a long time across the country and in California. A movement for mandatory prepayment of doctor and hospital expenses in the state commenced at the end of the progressive period, when in 1918 a prospective constitutional amendment empowering the legislature to start such an undertaking was defeated in the general election. Several probes by legislative committees, special commissions, and other groups were made in the twenties and thirties. The depression intensified the agitation. Even the Cali-

---

[4] *Sacramento Bee*, May 14, 1947, p. 4.

fornia Medical Association, in a rare burst of progressivism, endorsed the idea in 1935. The organization even sponsored legislation to that effect, ironically not too unlike that later presented by Warren. It was never passed. Soon thereafter the C.M.A. withdrew its endorsement and, as a defensive measure, introduced in 1938 its now renowned voluntary arrangement. This, christened the California Physicians' Service, was designed to accompany the famed Blue Cross hospitalization program. Warren's predecessor, Culbert Olson, sponsored an omnibus program that contained many features resembling those subsequently proposed by Warren. It was turned down by the lawmakers in 1939 and again in 1941.

Thus there was a large amount of background data on state health benefits prior to their incorporation into Warren's legislative agenda. However, for a Republican officeholder to advocate it, especially at that time, was extraordinary and obviously destined to "liberalize" his reputation. He could, of course, legitimately claim some Republican connection to that proposal. His party's 1944 national platform called for "stimulation by federal aid of state plans to make medical and hospital service available to those in need without disturbing doctor-patient relationships or socializing medicine,"[5] although there was no repetition of the thought thereafter. Still, it took the national Democratic party until 1952 to make even passing reference to a similar program.

The Governor began to advocate state health insurance in 1945, following discussions with group representatives interested in the subject—including doctors. He told the solons that private endeavors "had only scratched the surface" (the California Physicians' Service had drawn but 100,000 members in over six years) and that ". . . in spite of all our haphazard efforts the only people who are certain of receiving adequate medical attention today are those who are wealthy and those who are indigent and forced to accept public charity. The great mass of our people

[5] National Republican Party Platform, 1944, in Kirk H. Porter and Donald B. Johnson, *National Party Platforms, 1840–1956* (Urbana: Univ. of Illinois Press, 1956), p. 409.

—those who work for a modest income—are unable to pay for proper medical care when adversity strikes."[6] Warren's prospective statute (AB 800) sought the creation of a special fund through a 3 percent payroll levy, half each to be paid by employees and management, the fund to be administered by a part-time, broadly representative, eleven-member authority with a full-time manager.

The venture encompassed only those then earning between three hundred and four thousand dollars yearly and their dependents and exempted a number of classes, essentially those excluded from unemployment insurance coverage. Basically the arrangement was to embrace routine treatment by a physician or surgeon, certain additional consultation and specialist services, laboratory and X-ray tests, hospitalization up to twenty-one days per year for each sickness or injury (but not ambulance transportation), drugs, biologics, bandages, splints, and other supplies prescribed by a doctor, general nursing rendered in a hospital (but not that of private or special nature), and dentistry to the extent of extraction and correction of tooth and gum infections. None of those provisions were applicable beyond one year for any single infirmity.

Most significantly, California's doctors were at liberty to join the health insurance enterprise or not. There was to be no restriction on freedom of choice by doctors of patients and vice versa. The sole element of compulsion was to be the revenue payment. Indeed, existing private plans that gave at least the same protection at no higher prices were to be allowed to continue alongside the public system. Here again the Governor envisaged another milestone on the road of cooperative endeavor, this time between the state and the medical profession.

Warren's project released a flood of opposition from the California Medical Association and a countercampaign to boom enrollment in its own C.P.S.–Blue Cross complex. The doctors hired the celebrated Whitaker and Baxter public relations firm. Among other things, they condemned the gubernatorial pursuit as "socialism," said that "political medicine is bad medicine,"

---

6 *1945 Biennial Message*, p. 8.

and advertised the group's alternative as "the American way."[7] They shrewdly hit newspapers, opinion leaders, legislators, and constituents with publicity in building group, official, and mass sentiment favoring the wisdom of the status quo. Illustrating their old stratagem of moving from a defensive to an offensive posture, Whitaker and Baxter not only sold the voluntary approach generally but had the doctors sanction a legislative measure for state assistance to private programs (AB 1200), a bill that did not pass principally because of only halfhearted backing from organized medicine. Interestingly, however, membership in C.P.S. and Blue Cross rose rapidly, which the Governor had as a secondary goal to be accomplished through the stimulus of the mandatory system. In any case the famed husband-wife publicity team was provided a smaller-scale laboratory in which to pretest political maneuvers to be used when they were engaged by the American Medical Association in 1949 to help bury President Truman's national health proposal.

A joint statement bearing the names of C.M.A. President Lowell S. Goin and Phillip K. Gilman, president-elect, was released in February, 1945, through Whitaker and Baxter's Campaigns, Inc. It protested that "no matter what safeguards may be written into compulsory health insurance legislation, when the state collects the money and pays the bill, doctors for all practical purposes will become state employees and the private practice of medicine will end."[8] This immediate, intense, and well-advertised medical antagonism prompted a lively, at times excoriating, radio exchange between Warren and his adversaries unequaled in state history. The whole episode was another manifestation of the Governor's fixation on public relations to combat group influences and of his instinct for open reiteration of the facts (as he saw them) to the voters.

The Chief Executive's answer to the opening Whitaker-Baxter-C.M.A. assault was calm, starting with an explanation of his recommendation: "It does not compel anyone to receive any

---

[7] Carey McWilliams, "Government by Whitaker and Baxter," *Nation*, 172, No. 16 (Apr. 21, 1951), 366-69.

[8] *Sacramento Bee*, Feb. 19, 1945, p. 2.

medical care. It does not compel any doctor to treat any patient. It merely compels those who are entitled to medical care to make contributions to the fund for that purpose. The worker is not compelled to accept the service, but it is available for him if he desires it. . . . While a family of modest income can neither anticipate nor budget for medical needs out of regular income, it can afford the cost of insurance." He reminded his listeners that some employers had already devised their own arrangements, realizing that "efficiency in their plants depends upon the health of their employees. Out of the millions of people in need of medical care, there are hundreds of thousands each day of the year who are going about their work only partially capable of doing their jobs. They cost the employer real money. Proper medical attention could return them speedily to a status of efficiency." He perhaps revealed some personal anxiety when he declared "there are many mothers and fathers who have almost daily concern over the costs of medical services. It is present even when every member of the family is healthy. . . . All of us shudder when we hear stories of what the cost of illness has done to a friend or neighbor. Individually, we cannot help them. Collectively we can and that is what I am proposing."[9]

Unappeased, the C.M.A. replied two nights later through Dr. Stanley Cochems, executive secretary of the Los Angeles County branch. Claiming emphatically that the "Warren-C.I.O." (C.I.O. allies had introduced a measure nearly identical to the Chief Executive's) attempt at "state medicine" was "outrageously impractical" and would bring about higher taxes and new levies on business, Cochems advanced a familiar bromide: "Should either bill become law California could not compete industrially with other states. . . ."[10]

Having warmed to the challenge, the Governor took only a few days to censure this latest attack. He denounced Cochems' peroration as one designed to "terrorize and not convince . . . Strangely, he said nothing about the needs of the people. His great concern was over the burden it would cast upon industry

----

9 *Ibid.*, Feb. 22, 1945, p. 4.
10 *Ibid.*, Feb. 24, 1945, p. 4.

in competition with other states. Doesn't that have a familiar ring? Was not the same argument made when the principle of industrial accident insurance was established in this state thirty years ago? . . . How many fair-minded employers would now give up industrial accident insurance? The number would be infinitesimal, and so it would be with health insurance once it were firmly established." In fact, Warren affirmed, the Golden State's natural advantages and allurements, plus a hardy work force, would redound to the benefit of private enterprise and far outweight the "burden" of taxes for health insurance. The Governor closed his case in these broadcasts by recalling that "almost every hazard of life is protected by insurance, even those . . . as unpredictable as earthquakes, floods, and hurricanes. No one calls such insurance 'outrageously impractical.' . . . I believe there is nothing our state government could do to bring more happiness into the homes of our people than to spread the prohibitive cost of medical care and hospitalization for families of modest and low incomes. . . ."[11]

Dr. Goin had the last word in this war over the air waves. He charged that Warren's proposition was "hastily prepared and ill-conceived," one that he had allowed himself to be "stampeded" into submitting. The C.M.A.'s head was convinced that these gubernatorial machinations would eventuate in "government regimentation . . . I do not believe you want a medical O.P.A. in California any more than I do, but I believe we are headed very definitely in that direction if we adopt any of the compulsory health insurance bills now pending. . . . Can we afford state medicine in California? When I say afford it, I don't merely mean can we afford to pay the tremendous taxes which will result from it, even though the cost in dollars is staggering. I mean can we afford the social liability which will devolve upon us if we surrender one of our most precious personal liberties for the mess of political pottage which is promised us."[12]

The decisive legislative step on Warren's measure was taken

---

11 *Ibid.*, Mar. 1, 1945, p. 4.
12 *Ibid.*, Mar. 8, 1945, p. 4.

in the assembly's public health committee. During its often heated deliberations many witnesses were heard, pro and con governmental and private. The polemic ranged from profound questions of philosophy and the nation's health to more earthy programmatic details and matters of finance. Punctuating the debate were charges of deliberate falsehoods, of muzzling of witnesses by the committee, and that the whole idea smacked of communism.

Dr. Nathan Sinai, a pro-Warren spokesman, was interrupted in the midst of his recitation on potential premiums and benefits by Republican Assemblyman (later Speaker) Sam Collins. The Orange County solon was sponsor of the alternative plan to strengthen private insurance systems, drawn up largely by the California Medical Association. With a trace of saltiness in his voice, Collins queried the Michigan doctor about his educational background. Sinai replied testily that it was common knowledge he held his degree in veterinary medicine and indignantly denied that only physicians and surgeons were qualified to speak to the issue of medical economics.

Calm was momentarily restored, at least until the proceedings reached a pyrrhic climax on costs. Rebuffed in his efforts to compel legislative Auditor Vandegrift to publicly prove his allegation of a $100,000,000 annual fund deficit, Democratic Assemblyman Augustus Hawkins angrily charged that Vandegrift was being protected by the Republican majority. At that point a vote was quickly moved and Warren's proposal, along with that of the C.I.O., was beaten.

Interestingly, Warren's program had been suppressed in a body with an 8 to 5 Democratic edge. Yet its only backers were three Democrats, while three other Democrats were not present when the crucial vote was taken. All five Republicans, including chairman Fred Kraft and Assembly Speaker Charles Lyon, responded with a resounding no and they were joined by two Democrats.

Down but not out, Warren spoke up, in remarks that again manifested his style of legislative relations, by saying that he did not "feel the cause of health insurance is lost in this legislature. I believe that before this session is over, the legislature will recognize there is a tremendously important and serious problem involved in this issue and that it will do something substantial about it. . . . I have such a profound belief in the necessity for this legislation and such respect for the combined judgment of the legislators that I am convinced they will find some method of solution before the session adjourns." Regarding the committee's recommendation of an interim study of the question, that was "just a polite way of entirely avoiding the issue and chloroforming the legislation." Not only had that subject been more than thoroughly analyzed, but the interim investigation was itself becoming a tool for stopping progress.[13]

The Governor's collaborators in the assembly were determined that he would have another chance. They tried to bring his bill to the floor, but failed. On this critical maneuver, carrying with it one of the most personally revered pieces of legislation he would ever advocate, the Chief Executive was sustained mainly by Democrats and largely abandoned by his own party. Twenty-eight Democrats and only ten Republicans backed him by assenting to withdrawal of the measure. They were overruled by a coalition of twenty-nine Republican members and ten Democrats, a one-vote loss. This heavy Democratic approval was in part an echo of a prior endorsement from their state central committee chairman, William Malone. Malone's words once more underscored Warren's affinity with Democratic precepts: "Democrats in both senate and assembly ought to take an affirmative position on a workable health insurance program. If this coincides with the views of the incumbent Governor, it still is the program of the Democratic party."[14] Now growing more disheartened, the Chief Executive complained: "It is a pretty hard blow to a great cause when the assembly won't even let it be debated on the floor in the light of day." But, he mourned, "such is the power of the lobbies that have been against this legislation."[15]

13 *Ibid.*, Apr. 7, 1945, p. 1.
14 *Ibid.*, Mar. 6, 1945, p. 1.
15 *Ibid.*, Apr. 11, 1945, p. 1.

Warren thought he detected in the close roll call at least a flicker of life for the venture, or something like it. The result was a new decision to plug only hospitalization benefits, trusting that elimination of the other compulsory elements would mollify the doctors' fraternity. This optimistic expectation was quickly dashed, accentuated by the protest of C.M.A. president-elect Phillip K. Gilman: "It is . . . a subterfuge intended to permit the start of a system of government medicine in the hospitals, with the transparent intent of . . . bringing the medical profession under state regimentation at a subsequent legislative session—a poorly disguised piece of political trickery, designed to enable the advocates of state medicine to get one foot in the door now and another later."[16] Initially tabled by the lower chamber's public health committee, this new measure was the object of a fast discharge motion by Assemblyman Alfred Wollenberg, San Francisco Republican and principal author of the Governor's health insurance bills. Predictably the house turned it down, but with more uniform Democratic support than Republican. Twenty-three members of the minority party and nine of the GOP approved that stratagem; thirty-two Republicans and thirteen Democrats did not.

An interesting incident before the balloting caused a rare accusation against Warren, that he was guilty of interference in the legislative process. Wollenberg read a gubernatorial statement to his colleagues urging that this item be passed and suggesting that they might profit from a "full and impartial investigation" of improper lobbying. Speaker Lyon immediately berated the Governor for "putting *himself* in the position of lobbying for a bill which he has no right to do." Warren's retort was terse: "Of course I have advocated the bill, not by way of a lobbyist but as the chief executive . . . charged with recommending . . . measures which, in his opinion, are for the welfare of the people. I have never heard before that there was anything questionable about a governor sending a straightforward message to the legislature on any subject before it." Wollenberg

---

[16] *Ibid.*, May 28, 1945, pp. 1, 4.

defended the Chief Executive: "Apparently all the Speaker is interested in is having a governor who doesn't think or offer any constructive ideas . . . but who sits blithely by instead and lets his announced program be kicked around. The lobbying engaged in by the opposition . . . has been the strongest and heaviest I've ever seen. . . ."[17]

The sometimes strange workings of bipartisanship and the frequently dilatory use of the interim committee were again exemplified as the 1945 session ended. A body to examine the matter was concocted adroitly by Lyon to encompass not only a preponderance of anti-health insurance assemblymen but a Democratic margin as well. Any responsibility for inaction would thus fall ostensibly on Democratic shoulders. Not surprisingly, its later report withheld an endorsement from compulsory medical or hospital compensation.

The louder Democratic applause for Warren on the topic of health insurance in legislative halls was repeated, belatedly, in official state party circles. Said the 1946 platform: "We recommend . . . a prepaid compulsory health insurance system which will guarantee extension of adequate . . . care to the citizens of our state."[18] They repeated the thought in 1948 and again in 1952. Warren's own state GOP made no allusion to the subject throughout his tenure in Sacramento.

However, Warren persisted in raising the point. In 1947 and 1949 he offered his own propositions. In 1951 and 1953 he refrained from a direct endorsement and referred only indirectly to the problem, requesting the solons to resolve it somehow. He had been slowed down in these later years, chastened by several straight defeats. Furthermore, President Truman had by then instituted his national health insurance campaign, an undertaking with state-federal cooperative features that Warren welcomed so long as the states refused to perform individually. Thus consciousness and effort had largely shifted to Washington, although to no avail. In each instance in these subsequent

---

[17] *Ibid.*, June 5, 1945, p. 1.
[18] *Platform of the California Democratic Party*, adopted at state convention at Sacramento, July 20, 1946, p. 2.

years the bills embodying Warren's ideas were dealt the *coup de grâce* by assembly or senate committees under Republican control.

Thus Warren carried on a prolonged, if futile, battle for compulsory medical coverage. The legislative beatings he endured on that issue were consistently administered by coalitions consisting principally of his fellow Republicans. Nevertheless, his faith in the program remained unshaken throughout his governorship. This was well demonstrated in a 1951 speech, a talk that also accentuated his pragmatism. He did not accept "socialized medicine" but he did "believe in social progress, which has been the hallmark and glory of the American nation from the beginning. I am convinced we will enter upon a new era of progress in the cause of health when we make it possible for every one of our people to protect himself and his family from the economic disaster of back-breaking hospital and medical bills. I believe it is the responsibility of the states to undertake to help doctors, hospitals, and the public they serve in the solution of what, up to the present time, has been an insoluble problem."[19] Yet his overtures in the field, coupled with the efforts of President Truman, helped lay the groundwork for the present Medicare system through their data, arguments, and stimulus to public thinking on one of America's most perplexing issues.

The Chief Executive and Social Welfare

Contributing also to Warren's reputation for progressivism and independence as a Republican were his social welfare activities, an area of notable achievement for his administration. An alluring climate and an aura of limitless opportunity naturally drew to California a sizeable contingent of "senior citizens." Many of them were quickly added to public assistance rolls. Not unexpectedly, the state pioneered in aid to the aged.

---

[19] Address to American Public Health Association Convention, Oct. 31, 1951, *Warren Speeches.*

Its system was inaugurated in 1930, five years before federal money began to flow into the enterprise through the Social Security Act. Long sensitive to the burdens of the aged, the Governor turned his attention to them soon after taking office. He told the lawmakers that "our pension system should not be based upon . . . pauperism" but "upon social right. . . . The ultimate solution . . . will come through advances made on a national scale. Yet we should not permit this thought to delay our own efforts to build and maintain a pension structure within the limits of our ability to pay."[20]

Warren's words on the question further manifested his political posture: "No sound contribution can be made . . . without removing the issue from . . . politics and propaganda. There must be a correlation of all sincere thinking on the subject in order that we may move in unison toward the most practical goal obtainable. . . ."[21] To that end, Warren appointed a representative study committee to prepare a comprehensive report on the topic. Encompassing not only agricultural, business, labor, public, and service-club representatives but professional lobbyists for the elderly, the group may well have been too heterogeneous in makeup. For it could not abide by the gubernatorial injunction to "move in unison" in reaching its final conclusions. After nearly two months of one impasse after another punctuated by animated debate, a report was finally issued, endorsed by Warren and transmitted to the legislators. As a result, the maximum grant was raised, real and personal property allowances were liberalized, and relatives' responsibility was eased.

The Governor never asked for definite sums for the aged after 1943, typical of his frequent resort to generality in substantive matters. Nevertheless, he continually welcomed advances and signed into law periodic increases in the allowances. Such established undertakings as assistance to the aged, the blind, and needy children (as well as many other programs in the areas of health, welfare, and labor) were sufficiently accepted by then to command the automatic respect and action

[20] *Inaugural Address of January 4, 1943* (Sacramento: 1943), p. 12.
[21] *Ibid.*

of chief executive and solon alike. There was no compelling need for constant requests for specific amounts from the gubernatorial office.

Yet California's pension arrangements were steadily improved during Warren's governorship, mirrored in a doubling of the maximum stipend from forty to eighty dollars, the assumption by Sacramento of a proportionately heavier share of the combined federal-state-county outlay, and augmentation in property allotments. All the while the caseload continued to grow and by 1953 California led the nation by a wide margin in recipients of aged aid. In this as in so many other substantive fields, including help for the blind and needy children, Warren received virtually no positive guidance from national or state party sources.

California was also an innovator in assisting the blind. It established a program to that end as early as 1929 and later subdivided it into aid to those classed as "needy" and as "partially self-supporting." Here again Warren's aversion to specificity was evident, and he refused to be pinned down on details. Nevertheless, under him the state made steady progress on provisions for the blind. Its maximum allotment went from fifty to ninety dollars between 1943 and 1953, Sacramento's portion of the donation had rapidly accelerated and replaced that of the federal government as the heaviest, and property and other permissibles were raised. The caseload had climbed to second highest in the nation.

California's pathfinding welfare efforts are nowhere better exemplified than in ministering to impoverished children, a function that even predates those on behalf of the aged and blind. The 1879 constitution permitted services to indigent youngsters and a 1913 enactment under Hiram Johnson specified in detail those who might receive state sustenance. The definition of needy child was broadened under Warren's administration in 1949, wiping out the rigid classifications that had heretofore prevented many otherwise deserving young people from securing benefits. While progress was mainfest in this area too, it hardly compared with that made for the elderly and blind. A limitation had been put on the number of youngsters in any single residence who could obtain reimbursement, there was but slight elevation in property concessions, and the state portion of the contribution had declined. Still, California had the fastest increase in beneficiaries to cope with and stood first in family and child caseloads in 1953.

Assistance for the totally and permanently disabled between ages eighteen and sixty-five was amended into the federal Social Security Act in 1950, and the states were allowed to associate themselves with the undertaking by matching to a certain amount the grants of the national government. Warren immediately and wholeheartedly applauded the idea, opining that such benefits "should have been in the social welfare system a long time ago instead of putting disabled persons on general relief."[22] Despite his enthusiastic blessing before a special September session of the two legislative chambers that was convened well in advance of the October-first effective date for the new plan, his measure was killed in the lower house. Typical of the heavy Democratic support he had come to enjoy on bills of this type, sixteen members of that party made common cause with four Republicans in trying for a temporary rules suspension to remove it from committee. Twelve GOP assemblymen and one from the minority party went against that motion. It was lost for want of a mandatory two-thirds affirmative vote.

Far from discouraged, the Governor sponsored such proposals again in 1951 and 1953. His earlier recommendation ran afoul of the legislative auditor. The auditor's questioning of its financial feasibility helped sound its death knell in the assembly. Some twenty-six Democrats and sixteen Republicans approved it, but the bill was contrary to the wishes of twenty-six Republicans and three Democrats. It failed without the approbation of two-thirds of the total membership necessary to pass most appropriations. Warren's criticism of the pressures he thought responsible for this result was quick and spirited. He accused the state chamber of commerce, other organizations "within its orbit," and the state supervisors' association of being principally to blame. It was their "strenuous and callous" lobby-

---

[22] *Sacramento Bee*, Sept. 1, 1950, p. 8.

ing that had killed the bill. He proclaimed that such a service was inevitable in time and insisted that "all they accomplished was to wave back the tide." Concerning arguments he had heard that state social welfare provisions were already liberal enough, they were simply "as phony as any three dollar bill you ever saw." Indeed, refusal to enact the legislation was "acting retrogressively," when California was usually progressive in such matters.[23] To that time neither state political party had come out for or against public payments to the disabled. The Democrats gave it a ringing endorsement in 1952, a reflection of approval given as early as 1940 in the party's national convention. Warren's own GOP took no stand on the issue during his governorship, either statewide or nationally.

Thus, without Republican expression and more in accord with Democratic pronouncements on the subject, Warren made another appeal in 1953. He observed that thirty-four states, three territories, and the District of Columbia supplied such care and had compiled a total expenditure of only $67,000,000 for 1951–52. That was a long way from the "fantastic estimate of cost" of $100,000,000 then being circulated by the chamber of commerce. He emphasized that "all the large industrial states have instituted the program with the exception of California. If anyone in our society is deserving of the help of his government, it seems to me it is a needy person who is totally and permanently disabled. We must take care of them in some fashion, so why not do it humanely? I firmly believe that the people of our state will agree that it is a responsibility which should not be deferred any longer."[24] The state senate did not feel that way. It let his proposal expire in its social welfare committee, a body with a 7 to 2 Republican majority. Yet the Governor proved a trail blazer in this field. His 1951 prediction of inevitability came to pass when California launched such a system in 1957 under his successor, Goodwin Knight.

Because California has long been a haven for the aged, it has

---

[23] *Ibid.*, June 20, 1951, p. 10.

[24] *Message to the California Legislature, January 5, 1953* (Sacramento: 1953), p. 7.

likewise been a favorite breeding ground for full-time and shrewd pension advocates. There are many explanations for the naturalness with which the elderly have been organized and attracted to politics in the state. Relevant are such factors as a salubrious climate that baited many into retirement on small budgets, which they found difficult to balance during the depression decade, and a comparative lack of social stability or of settled channels through which mass protest might find an outlet—these exacerbated by a mountainous population boom, a basic richness that made poverty seem anachronistic, a history of forward-looking steps in welfare work, the conditioning effect these factors had on many executives, lawmakers, and office-seekers who eventually had to compete for votes among a growing bloc of oldsters, and a vigorous tradition of direct legislation.

The leading lobbyist and political provocateur for senior citizens during Warren's administration and for years following was the late George McLain. McLain was an inveterate and inventive promoter of causes for the underdog and a perennial candidate for assorted elective posts, and his suave personality, handsome countenance, and prodigious oratorical abilities roused the emotions and unlocked the pocket-books of many Californians, young and old. In 1941 he christened his California Institute of Social Welfare. This combination service organization and political movement not only helped pensioners secure every benefit to which they were entitled under existing law but also petitioned the solons for an ever better deal. In times past it had recurrently instigated proposition campaigns to that end. McLain's schemes appeared on the ballot periodically in Warren's day. They were methodically voted down, except once, in 1948. That incident unleased one of the more torrid episodes in state politics and ensnared the Governor.

Relations between Warren and McLain were relatively cordial when Warren first entered the executive mansion. Indeed, the "champion of the old folks" endorsed the Republican gubernatorial nominee in 1942, although more out of spite for Democratic incumbent Olson than affection for Warren. The new

Chief Executive, perhaps unwittingly, boosted McLain by naming him to his 1943 committee on old age assistance. The fact that the pension advocate found himself in disagreement with the majority report of that unit, endorsed by the Governor, did not deter him from taking a lion's share of credit for the outcome of its deliberations. His machinations strained whatever influence he had with Warren, and increasingly thereafter the two men squared off over amounts and administration of aid. They were so estranged by 1946 that McLain beat the drums for Democrat Robert Kenny for the statehouse that year. He repeated his performance with even more gusto on behalf of James Roosevelt in 1950.

Antagonism between the two reached its acme shortly after the polls closed in November, 1948. To the astonishment of almost everyone, the electorate had approved the now famous, McLain-contrived Proposition Four. It was amended into the state's already bulky constitution as Article 25. This conglomeration elevated the maximum monthly stipend to the elderly from sixty-five to seventy-five dollars, and in a gesture of appeasement to the blind (frequently bracketed with the aged, often to their chagrin), raised their top subvention from seventy-five to eighty-five dollars. Furthermore, many could now qualify for benefits at age sixty-three, personal property allowances were increased, and relatives' responsibility was eliminated entirely.

However, the stormiest legal modifications pertained to administration. All county functions were removed, including money donations, and Sacramento alone was made accountable for managing the system. Warren's social welfare director was summarily ejected from office and his position made elective with a four-year term. If that was not sufficient to anger the Governor and many of his associates, certainly sufficient was the stipulation naming a temporary head of that agency until a popular vote could be taken in 1950. Appointed to the job was none other than Mrs. Myrtle Williams, secretary-treasurer of McLain's group. Control over policymaking was taken from the board and vested exclusively in the new department boss. Additionally, a first lien on state funds was henceforth reserved for pensions. It replaced the traditional claim held by public education, something that turned out to be a political mistake of the first magnitude.

Once the new undertaking was voted in, California's political pot boiled over. Warren was relatively quiet during the 1948 contest, as he tended to be regarding campaigns other than his own. He was partial to a more liberal subsidy but was against the enterprise as a whole because of its other provisos and larger financial implications. Yet if he held his tongue before election day, he certainly did not after the returns were tabulated. Since the people had so acted, he lectured, surely they must have envisaged paying for any new expenses through more taxes. Accordingly, he asked the assembly and senate to terminate the reductions commenced under his administration in 1943 on bank and corporation franchise, corporate and personal income, and sales levies. They were also asked to hike liquor excises from $.80 to $1.50 a gallon, impose a two-cent-per-package assessment on cigarettes, and augment license fees on pari-mutuel betting. The lawmakers accepted his first recommendation but not those recommendations dealing with spirits, tobacco, and horse racing.

If the Governor was displeased, the California Council for the Blind was outraged. Its leadership resented the way McLain often used them to further his own causes, and they were incensed over some of Mrs. Williams' administrative orders. They decided to spearhead a repeal of the new law along with the chamber of commerce. In an astute strategy, the forces of the blind became the publicity vanguard for change and the more controversial but wealthier business group furnished most of the cash. When they had collected enough signatures on their petition, they asked the Governor to call a special election. Assailed from both sides, the Governor was told by McLain's allies that if he did effect that plebiscite, he would be a candidate for recall. In case he was toying with the idea, their electioneering arm, the Citizens' Committee for Old Age Pensions, was starting to sell buttons reading "Recall Warren to Save Pensions" for a dollar apiece. Warren fumed: "It sounds like a bulldozing scheme to me, and is typical of Mr. McLain's arrogance. I will not be coerced into making any decisions . . . at this time."[25]

Yet the Governor's hand was forced. No neophyte as a politician, he threw the issue to the legislature, since it was also allowed to provide for special referenda. Neither did the solons prove political amateurs. They set a test at the polls for November, 1949, ostensibly (or so they righteously intoned) for a popular verdict on a $250,000,000 school bond issue urgently advocated by the education people. If this meant that all propositions then qualified had to go on the same ballot, including the nullifier, that was not their fault. McLain's infuriated forces immediately declared war on the school proposal, before both the lawmakers and the electorate. Still enraged over the forfeiture of their privileged hold on the state coffers, the education bloc eagerly joined the fray with a full-scale assault on the pension status quo.

The state Congress of Parents and Teachers, the California Teachers' Association, the Supervisors' Association and the League of California Cities (the last two irritated over the loss of local responsibilities in the field), plus the League of Women Voters (concerned with administrative shortcomings and insertion of the McLain program into the state constitution), took the side of the blind and the businessmen. Some Democratic leaders even suspected that McLain was aiming for a takeover of their party. Indeed, there was talk of his gubernatorial ambitions against Warren in 1950. Still, the lobbyist for the old folks was not without allies in 1949, for most leaders of the A.F.L. and C.I.O. stood with him. The columns of his newspaper, the *National Welfare Advocate,* and his daily afternoon radio broadcasts, carried then by many smaller stations around the state, grew in rancor and emotionalism as he castigated the repeal and pleaded for money to defeat it.

Two incidents particularly hurt McLain during the campaign. One was a well-timed state Finance Department report in October that direly forecast $90,000,000 more in costs during

---

[25] *Sacramento Bee,* Mar. 8, 1949, p. 1.

the fiscal year of 1950 than would have been required prior to the plan's adoption. The second was an investigation by the Sacramento County grand jury that probed the link between McLain and Los Angeles Assemblyman John Evans, one of the Governor's prime foes on health insurance. It turned out that the legislator was on the payroll of the California Institute of Social Welfare with a clear conflict of interest. He made some amends by formally quitting the McLain organization, but it did him no political good thereafter. He was ultimately retired from public life in 1954 by a young aspirant that Californians would hear much more from in the future, Jesse Unruh.

As in 1948, Warren again declined to become too personally embroiled in the 1949 controversy. Still, his convictions were undisguised as he cast an absentee vote for revocation. At that time he charged that current arrangements were not in the best interests of the aged, the blind, "or any other segment of our people except the pension promoters who are now behind the scenes manipulators of our entire social welfare system. . . . The present setup even guarantees in the constitution that the legislature cannot interfere with this unconscionable exploitation. . . . The law now sanctions this chicanery and the divorcement from the normal operations of government leaves our entire system of social welfare susceptible to the manipulation of sinister and unseen hands."[26] The Governor welcomed a seventy-five-dollar maximum grant and pointed out that the repeal measure preserved that level while returning aged-assistance operations in all other respects to their pre-1949 pattern. Refixing the eligibility age at sixty-five and restoring relatives' responsibility would be the only things that would effect receipt of benefits for some persons. After one of the more tumultuous campaigns in California, the endeavors of McLain's antagonists and the sentiments of Warren were crowned with success on November 5, 1949. On that day the electorate brought to a close the sole experiment sponsored by the self-appointed spokesman for the elderly to have found its way into the law of the state.

---

[26] *Ibid.*, Nov. 2, 1949, pp. 1, 4.

Warren and Labor

Warren's nonpartisan proclivities and backing, his desire for cooperative endeavor, and his propensity for careful planning and measured progress were obvious also in the labor field. He gained no little electoral support from workers and the plaudits of many liberal legislators of both parties for his attempts to secure high employment levels and foster industrial peace, and from his sponsorship of improved benefits for working people. Indeed, the state Federation of Labor endorsed him for re-election in 1946. Its secretary-treasurer, Cornelius J. Haggerty, at that time said: ". . . as governor of California Earl Warren . . . has taken a principled stand on every vital question that has affected the interests of the citizens of California. . . . He has the courage of his convictions and the statesmanship to fight for them. A man of his stamp breeds confidence and respect even if you do not agree with him on every issue. Labor has nothing to fear from such a man. All labor wants is a fair umpire, and from our experience we know that in Earl Warren we have found such a man."[27] According to the federation, the Governor had compiled ninety-four favorable actions and only nineteen adverse actions on bills through the 1949 legislative session, based upon his signatures and vetoes.[28]

The indoctrination of family heritage was obvious here: "I come from a humble workingman's home. My father worked with his hands as a mechanic. Both he and I worked twelve hours a day, six days a week at twenty-five cents an hour. I know what better wages mean to a home. I know what better working conditions mean to the safety, health and well-being of all working people. I know what better hours mean to a family. I was never injured myself. But I have helped carry men from

---

[27] Address at launching of Warren campaign for re-election in San Francisco, Apr. 24, 1946. Copy in Federation Headquarters, San Francisco.

[28] California Labor League for Political Education, "Summary of Governor Warren's Legislative Record, 1943-1949," mimeographed, 1 page. Copy in Federation Headquarters, San Francisco.

the bench or lathe to have removed an arm or leg, crushed because of a lack of safety devices. As a boy, I knew good men blacklisted because they belonged to unions or participated in a strike. My nature always recoiled against these inequities. All my life, I wanted to see them wiped out."[29]

Warren took steps to guard against joblessness in postwar years shortly after he assumed California's highest office. He enjoined the lawmakers to lay the groundwork in 1943: "We must avoid a return to the dole. We must set ourselves to the scientific preparation of a backlog of construction projects which coordinate . . . the physical improvement of our state and the bolstering of morale through beneficial utilization of surplus manpower."[30] Cooperation was to be the watchword, for state government and private enterprise shared a joint obligation. Public planning and building provided "shock absorbers," means by which returning veterans and those released from defense plants could be kept occupied while industry retooled for peacetime production. In addition, they served to reshape the state's physical plant, neglected during depression and war. Over the next several years the Governor requested and won legislative inauguration of a number of special funds to finance postwar construction and to boost employment.

One interesting political episode concerned the "postwar unemployment and construction fund" of $90,000,00, established by the lawmakers in 1945 to assist the localities with their building plans. The following year the assembly and senate tendered the entire amount to the cities and counties, divided $45,000,000 apiece. Warren protested, hoping to extract some $34,000,000 for the state. He dubbed the proposal (AB 60) the Christmas Tree Bill, since there was "something in it for everyone."[31] Giveaway or not, it sailed smoothly through legislative halls. Meanwhile a $154,000,000 gubernatorial measure (AB 9), which also tapped AB 60 for the total desired by the Chief Executive,

---

[29] Address at Sailors' Union Building, San Francisco, Nov. 3, 1950, *Warren Speeches.*

[30] *1943 Inaugural Address,* pp. 11–12.

[31] *Sacramento Bee,* Jan. 15, 1946, p. 1.

encountered one setback after another. It was first amended in lower-house committee to prevent Sacramento from touching any of the money headed for the localities. Then in senate committee all prospective state expenditures were "line-itemed," rather than left in larger sums to be allocated at the administration's discretion. His bill thus decimated, Waren confessed despairingly that he was in "utter amazement at the apathy around this capitol building concerning the needs of the state institutions. . . . I don't see how any appropriation bill of major importance can be sent down to my desk without first giving consideration to the very deplorable conditions of our state institutions."[32] Undeterred, the solons passed AB 60. The Governor promptly vetoed it.

Many assembly Democrats came to the defense of Warren. Floor leader Alfred Robertson warned that Democrats of the lower chamber would vote to uphold the Chief Executive's rejection of AB 60 unless the Republican-controlled senate committee released AB 9 so that both could be considered together. The upper house unit quickly sent the administration measure to the floor with all "line-item" restrictions removed. Pressures intensified in favor of reversing the Governor's action on AB 60 as the day for the final roll call approached. Fred Alexander, executive secretary of the County Supervisors' Association, pleaded with his constituents to "let our friends in the legislature know that you . . . urge the over-riding of the Governor's veto."[33] Although the $154,000,000 measure was finally approved, Warren's blue penciling of AB 60 was also reversed. Here was clear evidence of the strength of California's "local interest" lobby and the influence of the home constituency on legislators. They also made history of sorts, for this was the only time a Warren veto was nullified in his nearly eleven years as chief executive.

Warren's fondness for teamwork and citizen participation in formulating the agenda of public business was evident in his 1943 overture, sanctioned by the lawmakers, for a Reconstruc-

---

[32] *Ibid.*, Feb. 1, 1946, p. 4.
[33] *Ibid.*, Feb. 11, 1946, p. 1.

tion and Re-Employment Commission. He discussed the motivations behind the organization's establishment before its membership. The new body should "devote itself primarily to . . . helping all individuals and groups . . . concerned with postwar problems to help themselves. . . . Real planning for material achievements . . . must come from the individuals and groups able to actually carry out the plans. No superimposed . . . agency . . . can ever take the place of individual and community effort. . . ." Nevertheless, "government itself has special responsibilities in these critical days."[34] The commission would inspire and facilitate state, local, and private projects. It would promote the rehiring of veterans and displaced workers, the conversion of industry to peacetime conditions, and the creation of new private businesses. The institution was to study California's human, natural, and economic resources in order to make information, recommendations, and aid available to public and voluntary bodies. Consisting as it did of a broad cross section of official and lay members, Warren borrowed freely from its suggestions through 1947, when the body was dissolved.

Further insight into Warren's political thinking was afforded by the full-employment issue that arose in the 1945-46 period. Denouncing the Chief Executive in 1945 for a "breadline" approach to postwar employment planning, a number of Democratic lawmakers and C.I.O. leaders pushed a measure more far-reaching in its commitment of state resources and gubernatorial action in the field. Objecting to certain of its features, in particular a provision to eliminate the Reconstruction and Re-Employment Commission, Warren refused to back the item and so did the legislature. The Governor was severely criticized by a number of prominent Democrats.

Partly in response to moves by the national Democratic administration that eventuated in the Employment Act of 1946 and to an expression of confidence in the idea by his own R.R.C., but primarily as a result of the 1945 encounter with California

[34] *Report and Recommendations of the California State Reconstruction and Re-Employment Commission*, period ending Dec. 31, 1944 (Sacramento: 1945), p. 1.

Democrats, Warren sponsored a full-employment program almost identical to theirs at a 1946 special session of the legislature which he summoned for that and other related purposes. Proposing a seven-man council named by the Governor to supervise the undertaking, the administration bill directed the agency to gather data and enlighten the chief executive on California's employment situation, its labor-force size and its production in all fields, the volumes of investment and expenditure needed to reach "full employment" by all government levels and the business community, the extent to which industry could absorb the supply of workers, and the percentage threatened with enforced idleness. This information would then be used for Warren's "production and employment" estimate to be submitted by him at each regular session of the legislature. It would contain a prognostication on the matters above and suggest public and nongovernmental projects. The new institution would serve as a corps of "economic advisers" to the administration, similar to the ultimate federal pattern established under President Truman.

In a January press conference on the topic the Governor reflected his penchant for meticulous planning and thorough understanding of the facts with these remarks: "Ours is the obligation to constantly find and assess the facts, to assume the responsibility for dealing with them in time and to protect our people as far as humanly possible. . . . Our production and employment problems have become so complex that it seems nothing less than dangerous for us to drift along on optimism and guesswork, improvising from day to day, without any means of detecting the underlying signs of the times until disaster is actually upon us. . . . The time has come for us to be realistic —factual—and to equip ourselves to get our present bearings and chart our future course. . . . In my opinion, government has the responsibility for doing it in a manner that will keep our government, our producers, our distributors, and our customers thoroughly and currently informed through the critical years ahead."[35]

---

[35] *Sacramento Bee,* Jan. 28, 1946, p. 1.

Nevertheless, Warren lost on the issue in the lower chamber —on another roll call showing concentrated Democratic support for him. Thirty-six legislators from the Democratic party and thirteen from the GOP were in accord with the Governor. The twenty-three dissenters, all Republicans, were sufficient to stop the item since it contained an appropriation necessitating approval by two-thirds of the total membership. Furthermore, the Chief Executive found himself in agreement with the Democratic state party's official position as well, reflected in its platforms of 1944, 1946, 1950, and 1952. Both state and federal branches of the GOP were utterly silent on the question from 1942 through 1952.

Earl Warren's personal principle of cooperative endeavor in the labor realm fit neatly into the atmosphere of unity in World War II. No time could be wasted on bickering between labor and management, strife that might cost the lives of American soldiers. Since partisan politics was to be adjourned for the duration, the two contending forces must also declare an armistice. Frequent meetings with union and business leaders under the Governor's tutelage became common practice. His convictions impelled him to advocate a continuation of that policy even after hostilities ended: ". . . we must repudiate once and for all any theory of conflict between those who organize business activity and those who work within it. The principle of collaboration must be substituted—a principle that has united us in war and that must be retained for the vital tasks of peace."[36]

A fitting occasion for practical application of this article of Warren's faith came in 1947 at the first regular legislative session in the postwar era. The point of compromise was an unemployment insurance bill (AB 1328, ultimately passed) which augmented maximum benefits from twenty to twenty-five dollars weekly. It also embodied a recommendation, first made by the Chief Executive in 1945, to prolong the permissible length of payments from 23.3 to 26 weeks. The state labor federation accepted an amendment allowing certain decreases in employer

---

[36] Address at Sacramento Host Breakfast, Sept. 9, 1944, *Warren Speeches*.

contributions in order to ensure its final approval. The Governor was jubilant at the signature ceremony: "This is an outstanding instance where labor and management have been able to reconcile their differences . . . and join in the enactment of a statute which will accomplish the objectives of both."[37]

Perhaps the most notable accommodation occurred in 1951 at Warren's invitation, once more under the sobering influence of national emergency during the Korean engagement. The Chief Executive chaired several discussions between federation and insurance company representatives, negotations that resulted in a revision of disability arrangements and workmen's compensation. In the area of disability, for example, AB 3376 in its original form tried to raise the top weekly grant from twenty-five to thirty-five dollars; a five-dollar increment and a number of other liberalizations were prescribed instead. In the interest of insurers, the new law made it easier for private firms to write such compensation. Each side dropped its sponsorship of an array of controversial projects as a consequence of this compromise. Yet Warren's call for compromise backfired to an extent in 1951. As a part of the "consensus," all except the Governor agreed that unemployment stipends for agricultural workers would not be advantageous.

In fact, the Governor's larger mission of securing harmony was only partially fulfilled. It was generally ineffectual at many legislative gatherings and at times deterred the very progress he so desired, progress that could be achieved only through the combat of rival groups. An overemphasis on concord for its own sake has its limitations and occasionally results in an emaciated policy product. Evidence of this abounded in Warren's last confrontation with the legislature in 1953, when the solons spent much of their time and energy putting aside labor legislation the Governor might think antagonistic or retaliatory. It was not surprising that he lamented the do-nothing attitude of the lawmakers in 1953. Indeed, a number of his own favorite

---

[37] *Sacramento Bee,* May 17, 1947, p. 1.

propositions were lost that year. Down to defeat went those designed to extend jobless subventions to farm laborers, domestics, and other classes, to raise unemployment, disability, and industrial-accident allotments, and to protect the solvency of these funds.

Nevertheless, Warren's striving for unity paid dividends to the unions in another context and earned him the gratitude of many of California's working men and women. It was in response to his entreaties that the state's legislators repeatedly shelved bills aimed at weakening labor organizations. These were various items that prohibited featherbedding, restricted strikes and mass picketing, and threatened the dreaded open shop, proposals that were consistently pigeonholed in committee. Here, too, the Governor's viewpoint on the subject of repressive labor proposals, as he labeled them, was more Democratic than Republican. The Democrats had some unpleasant words for such measures in their official state pronouncements of 1944, 1946, 1948, and 1950. The language they used in 1946 was most exemplary: "We oppose any legislation which will in any way abridge or weaken the right of labor to organize, bargain collectively, strike or to lawfully picket."[38] The stand taken by California's GOP was not nearly as vigorous.

Still, Warren allowed to become law two 1947 enactments considered "punitive" by the unions. In these instances "umpire" Warren's calls were looked upon as serious breaches of friendship by them, and they were to cost him political backing from the state federation leadership. One of these statutes removed a wartime-duration clause from an original 1941 act suppressing "hot cargo" and secondary boycott operations. They were now banned permanently in California's internal commerce. The bill was sponsored by Republican Senator George Hatfield of Merced, former lieutenant governor under Frank Merriam, and was zealously advocated by the California Farm Bureau, the state Agricultural Council, the Cattlemen's Association, and

---

[38] *1946 California Democratic Party Platform*, p. 4.

the ultraconservative Associated Farmers, who claimed the
measure was intended to foster the "unobstructed distribution"
of farm goods.

The Governor's strategy on the hot-cargo enactment was
unique. He let it go into force without his signature. He followed that course because of conflicting opinions concerning its
constitutionality—differences primarily between the legislative
counsel and the attorney general. Furthermore, litigation chal-
lenging the existing code provision was then pending before the
state supreme court. Warren's performance manifested his reverence for the popular will and for legal proprieties. He felt that
a veto by him, an action which he claimed to favor, would nonetheless deprive the citizens of an independent judicial determination of an act (the 1941 law) they had upheld in a 1942
referendum. Labor activists were somewhat mollified by the
high tribunal's subsequent ruling that the hot-cargo prohibition
was unconstitutional because some of its articles violated First
Amendment guarantees on free speech. However, nothing could
pacify them when Warren signed a 1947 statute forbidding
jurisdictional strikes.

The Governor chose the rather hostile environment of the
state federation's forty-fifth annual convention to unburden his
conscience, probably with great trepidation but with some
courage as well: ". . . the vast majority of the American people
are opposed to jurisdictional strikes. I believe the vast majority
of the members of your organization are opposed to them. They
help no one. They hurt everyone." He continued with language
that might well have been at the heart of his reasoning: ". . . their
continuance within the ranks of labor was swinging the pen-
dulum of public opinion against you. . . . I studied the bill care-
fully. I do not believe it is . . . perfect. . . . Most bills are not.
Neither do I believe it will result in any great injury to labor
unions." He again revealed his respect for the judiciary and for
the ultimate wisdom of popular action when he remarked: "I
have sufficient confidence in our courts to believe . . . that neither
this nor any other law will be permitted surreptitiously to wipe
out the rights of working men and women through organized

labor. . . . And if it should accomplish such a purpose, our people would change it to prevent such a result."[39]

Warren once more relied on the beliefs of a key Democrat by noting that President Truman, certainly no enemy of unions, was against jurisdictional strikes. The Governor was perhaps anticipating future opposition from the federation when he asserted that "honest difference of opinion, publicly expressed, grinds out its contribution to ultimate sound progress." He chronicled the many diatribes hurled at him by disgruntled interests over the years. They had come from oil companies for his sponsorship of highway construction through larger gasoline taxes, the medical profession on compulsory health insurance, and employer associations on improvements in unemployment benefits and workmen's compensation. He asked his labor audience to remember that "motives and objectives are the real tests of good faith, not single issues."[40] Yet his reasoning had fallen on many deaf ears, for his approval of the jurisdictional strike measure was a cardinal reason for the federation's refusal to repeat its 1946 endorsement of him for re-election in 1950. It backed Democrat James Roosevelt instead.

Warren's position on the hot-cargo and jurisdictional-strike issues was enough to dampen the labor organization's enthusiasm for him. His opposition in 1948 to a federation-sponsored initiative to reapportion the state senate closer to a population basis (soundly defeated in the November balloting) was sufficient to drown it. Here was a bit of historical irony. The future chief justice who would write the epochal 1964 decision ordering a reconstitution of both chambers in all state legislatures along numerical lines, of "one man, one vote," was an ardent defender of California's county-based senate when he was its governor. He rationalized it then by stressing the necessity for "balance" and preventing "antagonism" that might hinder progress in the state. It was his conviction, obviously developed from the

---

[39] California State Federation of Labor, *Officers' Reports and Proceedings of the Forty-fifth Annual Convention at Sacramento, August 4 to August 8, 1947*, p. 161.

[40] *Sacramento Bee*, Aug. 5, 1947, p. 4.

vantage point of a ranking executive in a diverse state, that the value of rural and back-area localities to California's economy and culture far exceeded their size. This was a stock, long-enduring, and valid argument. Warren also observed in 1948 that the arrangement of senate districts was in keeping with the federal system of representation. Here was another venerable and politically acceptable but legally incorrect premise with its basis in the correspondence of county to state in essentially the same manner as state to national government. Nevertheless, his ideas would be reforged in the crucible of time and by the press of wider events, as has happened to many statesmen and will to countless others in the future.

Still, Warren was sincere in his desire to prevent warfare between labor and management. He not only strengthened California's official mediation and conciliation services but in 1948 sponsored the creation of an industrial-relations commission to investigate and make recommendations concerning labor-management dealings without waiting for quarrels to develop. However, the proposal advanced only as far as referral to the assembly's Republican-controlled governmental efficiency and economy committee, perhaps symptomatic of the tighter bond between the Governor and Democrats on the topic. In 1950 the Democratic party's California platform called for a "state labor relations board to promote collective bargaining as a further means of diminishing the causes of industrial disputes."[41] Their GOP rivals never agreed with the idea, although the 1948 Republican national convention came close to an endorsement.

The Warren Administration's record on labor benefits was fairly impressive. Even more impressive were the bipartisan often heavily Democratic, votes given the Chief Executive by the lawmakers at many crucial junctures. California's unemployment insurance system was liberalized, although not in all areas sought by the Governor. There was a broadening of such specifics as waiting period, duration of stipend, and coverage by size of firm between 1943 and 1953. Yet while grant level increased, from an eighteen- to a twenty-five-dollar maximum

---

[41] *California State Democratic Platform,* Aug. 6, 1950, p. 14.

they did not do so by amounts sufficient to preserve the high rating California enjoyed in 1943 in comparison with the rest of the country. In fact, state improvements in nonfinancial features of the program were part of nationwide advances and either trailed them or preceded them only slightly.

Still, Warren championed a number of forward steps in the field. In 1949 he pointed to the undeniable utility of jobless compensation as a socially humanitarian and economically stabilizing element in American society. Nonetheless, he expressed anxiety over a prime fault in the program, for it did not protect many citizens who deserved it. To him, if such aid was sound for some, it was sound for all. Accordingly, in 1949, 1951, and 1953 he asked for its extension to agricultural workers, domestics, and employees of nonprofit corporations. Indeed, to ignore farm laborers was financially detrimental to many rural communities because it swelled their direct-relief rolls. The majority of lawmakers opposed him on all three occasions, although once again he had the sympathy of many more Democrats than Republicans. A 1949 assembly vote to include farm workers found twenty-two Democrats and one Republican answering aye. The Chief Executive lost this key item in his agenda almost solely because of his own GOP, a solid front of thirty-five Republicans joining three Democrats to beat it. It was largely the same story outside the legislature. California's Republican party did not even allude to broader eligibility during the entire period, although GOP national conventions endorsed the general idea as early as 1940. On the other hand, the state Democrats reflected similar thinking by their national officials in 1952 by asking that the categories of employees above be specifically accommodated. Each time their thoughts preceded gubernatorial suggestions.

California's unemployment allotments may not have risen quickly or high enough to satisfy many during the Warren years. Yet there was a 1946 enactment, one which the Chief Executive made a personal cause, that more than any other made the state program one of the most comprehensive. It gained for California an image of liberality that still persists. The Governor told an extraordinary legislative session in January that year that individuals needed jobless payments when ill more than when in good health and idled for merely economic reasons. Because the state was one of only four with mandatory workers' contributions to the unemployment reserve, these should be earmarked for the new expenses.

Warren was no innovator in this regard, since the idea of disability payments had been debated before. Ironically, it had even been proposed in 1945 by the California Medical Association, threatened then with wider compulsory health insurance. Its counterproposition to the Governor's medical bill contained such sickness benefits and the notion was embodied in other legislation that year. These measures were all defeated, the one by the C.M.A. failing mainly because the organization's sponsorship was halfhearted. Warren did not press for sickness allowances then, pushing instead for the omnibus medical prepayment venture. When this was rejected in the assembly in 1945, he characteristically tried for half a loaf in 1946.

The Governor denied that his new enterprise constituted health insurance in disguise. However, with some hairsplitting (and presumably a straight face) he announced that if a frontal assault on the problem of high physician and hospital charges was impractical, then the difficulty could be partially resolved by these new payments. Essentially, they would be an income supplement when people were unemployed for physical reasons. Referring to a C.M.A. resolution of January 7, 1945, he said in presenting his case: ". . . it is interesting to note that the medical profession, long in a position to observe the distress of families deprived by illness of the income of the breadwinner, has recognized the importance and need for a program of disability benefits." Even the American Medical Association " 'through it House of Delegates has consistently favored such insurance.' "[42]

The legislature consented to the undertaking, making California the second state (after Rhode Island) to launch a system of disability grants. It authorized participants to draw subsidie

---

[42] *Special Message to the Legislature* in California Legislature, 56th (First Extraordinary) Sess., *Senate Journal*, Jan. 23, 1946 (Sacramento 1946), p. 229.

up to twenty-five dollars weekly for as long as thirty-five weeks, a maximum that went to thirty dollars weekly before the expiration of Warren's governorship. All other features pertaining to coverage and administration were similar to regular jobless insurance. The management and a majority on the payroll of any firm could elect to admit those so voting to private plans in lieu of that run by the state, although their benefits had to be at least as great—a provision identical to one made in the 1945 medical fight.

In 1949 Warren reported that the new reserve was robust and growing steadily. The state's labor force was entitled to any worthwhile liberalization, since it provided the entire amount. Accordingly, the Governor (determined to get them one way or another) sought reimbursements for hospitalization. Unlike the original 1946 enactment, this proposition struck too near the doctor's collective nerve center for comfort. It immediately encountered their organized and irate resistance, bolstered by the antagonism of the chamber of commerce and the private insurance bloc. C.M.A. executive secretary John Hunton, an old foe of the Governor's on health insurance, pleaded for the measure's repudiation. He held that it would shift the disability arrangement from one of wage-loss indemnification to compulsory hospital compensation, destroy voluntary insurance plans, and be "an entering wedge for socialized medicine."[43]

Warren took a familiar step when his bill stalled in the legislature, turning to his constituents in one of his celebrated radio "Reports to the People." He described the facts of his proposal and voiced hope that popular pressure upon the two houses might impel them to act favorably. He also sharply censured his adversaries. The public fund had built up a surplus of $85,000,000. Surely, he said, insurance companies had been reaping correspondingly huge profits. If the state could afford this reform, so could the insurance firms. As for the doctors' brotherhood labeling it socialized medicine, that was "a rather fantastic claim and one that ill becomes that great profession," especially since it had already sanctioned the basic idea.[44]

[43] *Sacramento Bee*, Apr. 28, 1949, pp. 1, 4.
[44] Broadcast, May 3, 1949, *Warren Speeches*.

Thanks partly to his resort to pressure through public relations, Warren was ultimately triumphant on the issue after a number of setbacks in the legislature. Hospitalization stipends were set at eight dollars daily for a limit of twelve days, and regular disability grants could be collected in addition. The final upper-chamber roll call showed a slightly higher percentage of Democratic than Republican support for the gubernatorial position. Eleven Democrats locked arms with fourteen Republicans to pass it, while two Democrats and seven Republicans protested. By July 1, 1953, California was one of four states with sickness and injury allowances; it was the only state in the country with hospitalization payments.

Given his solicitude for the well-being of the state's laborers, it was logical that Warren should propose and lend his name to a number of improvements in California's long-established industrial-accident program. The Governor was rarely very definite in his overtures on the topic, although he recurrently asked the solons for advances. His words in 1949 were illustrative: "I recommend that our workmen's compensation . . . benefits be reviewed in the light of present living costs, and particularly, that the death . . . provision be reviewed for the purpose of making better provision for a widow during . . . her children's dependence. . . ."[45] His statement followed a 1948 endorsement by California's Democrats of an increase in both basic grants and death subsidies, and benefits for dependents. The Governor's own state GOP had no comment on the issue throughout his tenure.

In 1949 Warren told the legislators "the time has come when consideration should be given to the inclusion . . . of the groups that are now excluded. . . ."[46] A bill to spread the cloak of protection over all but a few employees was narrowly defeated in the lower house. A 31 to 34 count found a sizable ratio of Democrats in line with the Chief Executive's thinking. Twenty-four of their assemblymen and seven Republicans cast their lot with

---

[45] *Message to the Legislature, January 3, 1949* (Sacramento: 1949), p. 10.

[46] *Ibid.*

him. Five Democrats and a rousing twenty-nine members of the GOP were dissatisfied with the point. In 1951 and 1953 also, Warren tried to get the lawmakers to stretch industrial-accident stipulations to encompass other classes, especially farm laborers and domestic servants. Again he was repulsed.

Characteristically, the Governor refused to specify dollar figures in petitioning for raises in workmen's compensation. There was a general upward movement in the detailed and incredibly complicated categories of benefit during his terms of office, although the ranking of California as compared to other jurisdictions had substantially decreased in some aspects. By no means could the state be classed generally as a nationwide leader in workmen's compensation when Warren departed for the Supreme Court, despite some changes for the better. Indeed, there were no real innovations during his tenure in Sacramento, such as disability grants under unemployment insurance. Perhaps the disappointment expressed by the state Democratic party in its 1952 platform best summarized the feeling of many: "California's present . . . act is archaic. Its disability rating system requires continuing revision. We need speedier processing of claims and increased benefits to injured workers. We recommend early enactment of a new workmen's compensation act modeled on the most advanced acts of other jurisdictions."[47]

Warren received many legislative abstentions from treating problems of racial discrimination, particularly in employment. He resigned in 1953 without having secured his long-cherished goal of a state law preventing prejudical treatment of minorities. The Chief Executive's proposals in this area included both a suggested fair employment practices statute with enforcement powers, and entreaties for study and publicity of the issue to supply the facts necessary for further avenues of attack. His first recommendation came in 1945 and embodied the more conciliatory approach for a commission on political and economic equality. This body would investigate difficulties encountered by individuals due to their nationality, not only in seeking work

---

[47] *Platform of the California Democratic Party*, adopted at state convention at Sacramento, Aug. 21, 1952, p. 35.

but in exercising their political and social rights. It would give a yearly accounting to the governor and legislature. However, the measure was allowed to die in the assembly.

In 1946 the Governor came out for a full F.E.P.C. law, and in so doing found himself in agreement with the official Democratic position in California in this one instance. The state GOP never endorsed that particular proposal during the Warren years, although it did support the milder version. Warren said to the lawmakers in 1946: "California is a cosmopolitan state. Here the United Nations Charter was born. The Charter is based upon the protection of human rights, the most fundamental of which is the opportunity to earn a living. . . . I recommend that you enact legislation which will guarantee economic opportunity through a fair employment practices act."[48]

Three quite similar bills incorporated the Chief Executive's bid for action. They would have made it illegal for companies with five or more persons on their payrolls to discharge or refuse to hire anyone because of race, religion, color, national origin, or ancestry. Unions would also be forbidden to exclude or expel people on these grounds or to segregate their membership, and the measures were applicable to public agencies as well. The compelling force behind these prospective statutes would be a five-man commission which would probe allegations of unfairness and attempt initially to eliminate unlawful conduct by persuasion. Barring that, it could promulgate cease-and-desist orders when injustices were verified through a hearing. As a last resort it might obtain a court decree instructing compliance with its decision.

Two of these items were held in committee until final adjournment, although the other was withdrawn at one point from the assembly ways and means panel. Heavy Democratic backing for the Governor was again evident, as thirty members of that party and twelve Republicans sided with him by voting to dislodge that measure for floor consideration. Twenty-four Re-

---

48 *Message to the Legislature*, in California Legislature, 56th (First Extraordinary) Sess., *Assembly Journal*, Jan. 7, 1946 (Sacramento: 1946), p. 72.

publicans and three Democrats said no. However, the bill subsequently died without further action. With the Democratic
gubernatorial nomination as well as his own safely tucked under
his belt, the Chief Executive sanctioned an identical proposition
on the general election ballot that year, but it was defeated.
This was his last clear-cut advocacy of total F.E.P.C. in California.

Practical and realistic in dealing with public problems,
Warren in 1947 reverted to the more moderate civil rights device
he had sponsored in 1945. He continued to advocate it through
1953, although he was always sympathetic to and ready to accept a stronger alternative. Thus he remained closer to official
GOP state views on the topic during most of his administration.
Nevertheless, he was turned down at each legislative session,
ordinarily by the upper-chamber committee on governmental
efficiency and economy or by its assembly opposite. Both had
heavy Republican majorities from 1947 to 1953.

Californians discovered that Warren still had a fondness for
pure F.E.P.C. through his presidential candidacy in 1952, when
he welcomed a national statute so long as the states did not
have their own laws. The man who wrote the historic 1954
school-desegregation decision said there were two reasons he
felt that way: "First, it is my firm belief that the basic purpose
of our government is to insure equal opportunity in life for
Americans of every racial origin and creed. Second, the Republican party and those who have attained public office under
its standard and platforms are honor bound to support such a
law. I know there are Republicans who recoil at such a suggestion, but I would ask them if they have ever read their recent
[national] party platforms."[49]

Warren's second point had real meaning, for GOP national
conventions addressed themselves to the subject throughout his
years in the executive mansion. As early as 1944 they promised
to work for federal legislation establishing a permanent fair
employment practice commission. They apparently were trying
to win over disenchanted Democrats when they backtracked in

---

[49] *Sacramento Bee,* May 28, 1952, p. 8.

their 1948 and 1952 statements. In 1952 they claimed that the prime duty lay with the states, supplemented by appropriate federal pursuits. The national Democratic conclaves stressed justice for minorities in the armed services, in elections and politics, and in the economic realm. Yet because of southern pressures they did not commit themselves to F.E.P.C., as their rivals had done in 1944.

Since both parties had long professed such humanitarianism and because the 1952 GOP stance was essentially one for state initiative, Warren took them at their word and in 1953 exhorted California's lawmakers to do "whatever is necessary" to wipe out racial inequities. Once more they denied him. The Republicans who dominated the assembly committee on governmental efficiency and economy were unable to follow their party's national planks on civil rights, as they pigeonholed a series of anti-discrimination proposals. However, here again Warren proved something of an educator and trail blazer. His gubernatorial successors fought for such legislation, and a full F.E.P.C. was ultimately put into California's legal codes in 1959 under Democratic Governor Edmund G. Brown.

Thus, as California governor, Earl Warren sought to bring to fruition his commitment to social progress through sponsorship of and assent to a number of programs and innovations in the fields of health, welfare, and labor. The level of achievement was not always as high as he had aimed, or at least hoped, for —and neither was the degree of support for his measures from his fellow Republicans in legislative and formal party circles. Yet he never ceased in his endeavors to convince them of the correctness of his convictions, not only as means for attaining the loftier goal of a better life for Californians and Americans generally but also for the more mundane, yet essential, end of electoral victory as well.

Earl Warren, the California Governorship, and the Supreme Court

PART FOUR

Earl Warren, the California Governorship,
and the Supreme Court

CHAPTER VI

Earl Warren: Social Progress, and Republicanism

Political Strategy or Fundamental Principle?

An interweaving of fundamental principle with political adroitness in Earl Warren's public demeanor was unmistakable in his exhortations to fellow Republicans to welcome social progress. The subjects discussed in their platforms were essentially nonpartisan since they were human considerations calling for governmental performance on behalf of all citizens: "The Republican party rose to a position of influence in our nation because it found the words and ideas which expressed the hopes of the average man for unity and action. This conception of party responsibility is fundamental to political effectiveness. It is essential to the continued progress of California."[1] The Governor took his plea to various GOP bodies during his 1952 presidential effort. The party would have to abide by such thinking if it was to live up to its own best traditions, do justice to its official policies, and be successful at the polls.

For one thing, only by subscribing to social progress would present-day Republicans be worthy of the Lincoln heritage. Warren asserted in a Boston speech honoring the birthday of the Great Emancipator: "Social progress was Lincoln's creed, and those who confuse it with socialism today are indulging in the kind of thinking that Lincoln described as not being able to

---

[1] Radio Address to Republican State Party Convention, July 20, 1946, *Warren Speeches.*

distinguish between a horse chestnut and a chestnut horse." The
Chief Executive condensed his own stand into the following
maxim: "I am a slow walker, but I never walk backwards."[2]

In fact, the party had adhered to such a concept in its recent
national declarations. The Governor stressed that "these plat
forms set forth clearly a doctrine of social progress. It has served
as a guidepost to me here in California and has assisted Repub
lican government in this state to fashion forward-looking and
progressive laws. I confess to amazement and even a bit of
irritation when occasionally someone accuses me of not follow
ing Republican doctrine."[3]

Warren urged the GOP to adopt a "liberal" posture in 1952
defining what that entailed: "By this I mean a platform that is
oriented to the problems of everyday American life—and for the
solutions of the problems that will make life better for the
American people. . . ." Nor was this mere political expediency
for those who mouthed "progressivism" and then failed to per
form accordingly could be legitimately criticized: "To me it is a
sad commentary that when the election is over, a great many of
our Republicans are of the opinion that, from that time on, we
should forget those platforms and do just the opposite of what
they advocate. Those people are inclined to call those who would
follow the platform 'me tooers.' . . ." The Governor's own reputa
tion in this regard stemmed simply from the fact that his admin
istration in California was dedicated to "carrying out the liberal
platform of the Republican party."[4]

Electability was also a cardinal ingredient, and Warren
warned Republicans that the only road to electoral triumph was
through social progress. He cautioned the state central com
mittee in 1951 that the GOP "must not—as it values its life—
become a party of reaction." It must occupy that area between
extremes of left and right: "Some people, becoming impatient
with the rate of progress, espouse some fanatical cause or adopt

---

[2] *Sacramento Bee*, Feb. 13, 1952, p. 1.

[3] Address to Republican National Committee Luncheon, Jan. 17, 1952
Warren Speeches.

[4] *Sacramento Bee*, Oct. 10, 1951, p. 8.

foreign ideology that by distance lends enchantment to them. Others resist all change as being fraught with danger. They hark back to the days when our country was small and economy simple—when government touched only very lightly the lives of our people. It is between these two groups—not with either of them—that the Republican party must pursue its course if it is to recruit new adherents; if it is to appeal to the great mass of voters who demand that progress be made in the solution of their individual problems which in the aggregate constitute the problems of our day."[5]

Warren used language that was prophetic for him personally when he noted that although the GOP had little trouble with a radical left wing, it did have its troubles with extremists from the right—"those who would freeze our nation to the status quo with whatever inequalities go with it and those who would have our country return to what they look back to nostalgically and affectionately call the 'good old days.' "[6] These individuals were not so numerous as they were vocal and influential. Yet the party would again sustain defeat unless such thoughts were repudiated.

His partisan aloofness and his advocacy of progressive measures brought forth no little condemnation of Warren from Republican conservatives. The same assertion made by Democratic Assemblyman Collins in 1945, that the Chief Executive was "trying to out–New Deal the New Deal," was uttered in 1946 in quite a different tone. In this instance it was an indictment, brought by Earl Lee Kelly, banker and former public works director from 1935 to 1939. Kelly lamented: "The tragedy of our present Republican state administration is that its policies are so akin to those of the C.I.O.–P.A.C. and all the radical riff-raff elements of California that it is difficult to find an issue on which Governor Warren and Robert W. Kenny, the probable Democratic nominee, are in serious disagreement."[7]

The banker dropped a not too subtle hint that he might challenge Warren in the primary: "If our party's chosen officials are

[5] *Ibid.*, Nov. 17, 1951, pp. 1, 4.
[6] *Ibid.*, Jan. 17, 1952, p. 1.
[7] *Ibid.*, Feb. 1, 1946, p. 4.

too cagey or opportunistic to go into battle wearing the party's colors, then we must either get new leaders or get ready for receivership. If Governor Warren intends to ride into battle with one leg astride the Republican elephant and the other clinging affectionately to the Democratic donkey, I can't help but wonder if either animal will recognize him as master."[8] For all his complaining, Kelly declined to contest Warren at the polls.

Local GOP groups occasionally sniped at the Governor. A gathering of some five hundred Southern California Republicans in November, 1948, assailed his "nonpartisanship" and "New Dealism," an action prompted partly by the party's startling and discouraging national election loss, with Warren as the vice-presidential running mate to Thomas Dewey. The disgruntled Republicans charged that the California GOP was a "monstrous patchwork quilt of an organization which serves only one individual in the state." Interestingly, they demanded elimination of cross-filing (a dream of many Democrats then and one that would ultimately come true once they gained power) so that candidates might be nominated who "subscribe to the principles of real Republicanism."[9]

The most celebrated rebellion against Warren by party tories came in 1952 in the presidential primary, the only time they threw down the gauntlet to him in a direct popular confrontation. The Chief Executive's adversaries rallied behind a nominal aspirant, Representative Thomas H. Werdel of Bakersfield. This so-called Independent Republican Delegation was highly sympathetic to the White House hopes of either General Douglas MacArthur or United States Senator Robert A. Taft. However, it was more anti-Warren than anything else. The Governor claimed that behind Werdel lay a number of his political enemies and assorted malcontents. Included were certain oil interests which harbored grudges over his sponsorship of highway expansion defrayed through gasoline and oil taxes; doctors who were still angered about his recommendations for public health insurance; disappointed office seekers; and party politi-

---

[8] *Ibid.*, Oct. 3, 1945, p. 4.
[9] *Ibid.*, Nov. 18, 1948, p. 17.

cians displeased with his independent decisions and philosophy
of government.

Warren's antagonists insisted that he was guilty of "Tru-
manism" and "creeping socialism," was proportionately "out-
spending and out-taxing the national administration," was a
Republican "only by registration," had been tabbed an "outstanding governor" and "a Democrat who doesn't know it" by
none other than Harry S. Truman, and had attempted four
times to "socialize California medical practice."[10] The Governor's
friends had some fun with the last allegation by pointing out
that the Werdel group was chaired by Edward H. Tickle, former
Monterey County state senator. In 1935 Tickle had authored the
compulsory health compensation bill then being advocated by the
C.M.A. Regardless of the intensive and expensive fight waged
by his foes, Warren's popularity with the state GOP voters remained essentially intact. He won the balloting by a two-to-one
margin in this last electoral contest before his appointment as
chief justice of the United States.

Earl Warren and Party Politics

Political parties perform a number of vital functions in the
United States. They crystallize opinion on candidates and issues,
inform the electorate and furnish it with ordered policy alternatives, and provide rational political responsibility once in power.
There is validity to the contention that Earl Warren's individualism considerably weakened these important mechanisms in
California. The chief executive is the state's highest officer.
Warren was its nominal Republican leader, and his indifference
to partisan affairs was bound to contribute to impairment of the
party. A potential and crucial source of central direction was
thereby weakened. Absence of strong partisanship from the
Governor helped to divert popular concentration and awareness
from party activities, given the publicity to his functions. Such
political practices by a chief executive were particularly un-

10 *Ibid.*, Feb. 20, 1952, p. 8.

fortunate in California, where parties were already defectiv

Yet contrary reasoning is not without credence. The state
parties were impotent long before Warren went to Sacrament
If any one man can be blamed for their debility it would have
be Hiram Johnson, for it was under his instigation and supe
vision from 1911 to 1917 that the legal foundation was laid f
the subsequent "nonpartisan" system. Inclined personally to c
so anyway, Warren simply availed himself of conditions as l
found them by utilizing tactics to draw Democrats and offs
their numerical superiority. In this way he was merely adjustin
to a key canon of politics—survival.

Indeed, the Governor may have indirectly strengthened h
party for the future: in practice in the short run, and by wa
of historical example for later years. His stratagem of nonalig
ment and commitment to social progress constituted a meanin
ful education for ambitious Republicans in California, an
elsewhere where circumstances were similar. It permitted captu
of high office by one affiliated with the party who represented
minority of the electorate. Goodwin Knight was his disciple
this regard. The fact that Warren was able to win and hold th
governorship, and to administer it well, redounded to the crec
of Republicanism generally in the state.

Warren's liberal outlook encouraged that strain of thoug
within Republican ranks. It assisted in recasting the GOP fro
a solidly conservative force in state politics when he went to th
capitol into a more moderate entity by the time he departed f
Washington. I am convinced that an organization largely of th
stamp is what Republicans will need in years to come if the
strivings for power are to be broadly realized. This is especial
true in California and in other big industrial and urban state
although admittedly not the case in every section and locali
of the country.

Warren helped to direct the national party along progressiv
lines by fostering such a viewpoint in one of the largest state
The moderate-liberal faction of the GOP dominated its pres
dential nominating politics from 1940 until 1964 and capture
the presidency with Dwight D. Eisenhower in 1952 and 195

he only such Republican victories from the twenties until 1968. Warren was a local forerunner of what the General and his aides were fond of calling Modern Republicanism, exemplified today by men like Governor Nelson Rockefeller, Senator Jacob Javits, Mayor John Lindsay, Senator Clifford Case and former Senator Thomas Kuchel.

The two principal American parties have generally moved closer together in their avowed beliefs since the thirties. Successive elections after 1932 ratified the innovations of the depression decade. As Key puts it: "A Republican victory in 1936, for example, would have braked the New Deal to a halt and probably resulted in the repeal of its major measures. A series of Democratic victories demonstrated majority acceptance of the Rooseveltian reforms and time brought Republican recognition of that fact. By 1952 the policy differences between the parties had become far narrower, and the practical consequences of a Republican victory in 1952 differed radically from those of 1936."[11] Warren unquestionably perceived the drift of this transformation and the extent to which people, both in California and nationwide, concurred in the liberal Democratic achievements of that era. He was thoroughly persuaded that Republicans throughout the United States should accept these past gains and build upon them, if they were to be at once shrewd politicians and useful public servants.

Party membership in the United States is not a binding arrangement, acts of affiliation being in most states routine and uncomplicated matters. Allegiance can be switched or registration permitted to lapse with comparative ease. The process consists more in a loose, over-all conviction than in a formality. Each side has its stalwarts who meticulously toil for the cause and others who methodically troop to the polling booths to mark their "X" for the entire ticket each time. Still, a very substantial percentage of voters (obviously varying with time and place) have only nominal loyalties. Thus party authorities and functionaries have long preoccupied themselves with attracting the

---

[11] V. O. Key, *Politics, Parties, and Pressure Groups*, 5th ed. (New York: Crowell, 1964), p. 225.

political agnostics, the relatively uncommitted, and the wavering to their respective banners. Warren's entire approach in California was geared toward that end and it proved most fruitful.

Political desires and grievances in the United States, if they are to have any effectiveness, must be channeled through one of only two parties. The electoral system of winner-take-all, historical traditions, and the American mental set dictate this elementary fact of politics. Each of the major parties is therefore driven by reality to make overtures to men and women of all social and economic gradations in this huge and heterogeneous land. As a result the Democratic and Republican aggregations are tremendously diverse in membership, and their internal diversification has had a moderating effect upon both doctrine and national leadership. A balance must be struck between divergent and often warring elements. Surely these obversations are also applicable to sprawling and conglomerate California during Warren's administration—a California then, as now, a cross section of the country in microcosm. The Governor was fully aware of the disparate constitution of his own party in the state. He hoped that his political behavior would not only add to its strength by winning over disenchanted Democrats and independents but might draw together different factions of the GOP behind his personal stewardship.

Most students of the subject agree that the paramount goal of American political parties is to secure the machinery of state, to acquire dominance at any given level of government by placing their standard-bearers therein. Many partisan activists may desire thereby to further a set of larger interests or broad policies. However, taking effective command of the apparatus of government is the immediate objective that consumes their time, money, and energies. Penniman has noted that "two great parties exist in America, not because there are two sides to every question but because there are two sides to every office—an outside and an inside."[12] Bone has said: "The basic motivation of each major party is to capture control of the government, and

---

[12] Howard R. Penniman, *Sait's American Parties and Elections*, 5th ed. (New York: Appleton-Century-Crofts, 1952), p. 153.

the contest between the two parties is a struggle for power rather than a contest between rival principles."[13]

Earl Warren fully appreciated the overriding aim of United States parties. He too was motivated by a yearning for electoral victory, with winning and holding a crucial position. This was the first order of business, the inescapable priority. And it had to be accomplished in conformity with the circumstances prevailing in California at that time. A triumph in the balloting is an absolute prerequisite to implementation of program for any office seeker. Warren enjoyed a high degree of good fortune at the polls; consequently he remained in office so that a considerable portion of his projects went into the statute books, even if not all of them did and some were passed with details not of his first choosing.

The two principal party platforms indulge in generalization and have frequently borne a striking resemblance to each other on many topics. They are intended to rally around the respective nominees as widespread a following as possible. Generous leeway is thus allowed their officeholders in propounding more definite recommendations based upon suggestions from other sources. Warren was conscious of the secondary nature of the party's policy-proposing function and capitalized upon that situation. It was partly for that reason that he could claim to be abiding by Republican doctrine, as enunciated in national GOP declarations, and relying upon it as a standard for official performance in California. Nonetheless, a scrutiny of state platforms during his administration indicates that those of the Democrats on balance contained more specific plans for public action and were closer than Republican affirmations to Warrens' record on many points. The Governor's programs also bore a close resemblance to many planks in national Democratic platforms.

The task of originating policy details has fallen mainly to organized interests. This practice was most conspicuous in California during the Warren years, given the decrepitude of the state's political parties. Certainly the Chief Executive recognized

---

[13] Hugh A. Bone, *American Politics and the Party System*, 2d ed. (New York: McGraw-Hill, 1955), p. 273.

that fact, for he has few peers in California history in tapping group representatives for possible legislation. He believed firmly that no single or limited segment of opinion had exclusive possession of the facts or of answers to public questions. Thus he probed a number of disparate viewpoints, illustrated most obviously by his citizen conferences, committees, and commissions.

Pervading American society is a popular expectation that partisan battles will be conducted with the objective of preserving solidarity rather than intensifying conflict. Lubell phrases it well: "In our history no party has been able to gain or hold ascendancy as the normal majority in the country unless it made itself the effective instrument for unifying the nation."[14] Most of our party chieftains try to picture themselves as dispensers of compromise among the many elements of society. V. O. Key has drawn our attention to the fact that "selections from the campaign oratory of Franklin D. Roosevelt and Dwight D. Eisenhower have a remarkably similar ring. Both on occasion placed emphasis on the interrelations of the interests of farmers, workers, businessmen, bankers, all of whom had common cause in the achievement of great national purposes. And to a degree party victory represents the victory of a conception of national purpose, not the undiluted triumph of a particular interest."[15] Warren's behavior showed that he was cognizant of this feature of American political culture. He perpetually endeavored to instill a "spirit of unity" in the California populace and hoped that electioneering might also serve that end.

Most American voters are highly candidate-oriented, more often competent to judge human qualities and abilities than the technicalities of civic issues. Consequently, our two biggest parties have to think largely in terms of personality and only secondarily about policy. Here again Warren displayed his alertness to a bedrock trait of partisan rivalry in the United States. He kept his gubernatorial campaigns entirely separate

---

[14] Samuel Lubell, *Revolt of the Moderates* (New York: Harper, 1956), p. 17.

[15] Key, *op. cit.*, p. 221.

from those of other GOP hopefuls and stressed his own independent accountability. This was done for good reason in California's free-wheeling political environment of that time, where the individual qualities of aspirants were all the more prominent.

Thus, perhaps Earl Warren grasped better than most politicians the facts of American public life, particularly as they applied then in California. When one thinks about the nature and purpose of parties in this country and the character of their competition, as they actually are and not as they should be in the view of some, he might well conclude that the Golden State's longest-tenured Governor was a better partisan than his record otherwise seems to demonstrate.

California has experienced a rejuvenation of competitive two-party politics and an increase in partisanship since Warren took his leave for the Supreme Court in 1953. The elimination of cross-filing, the rise of forceful and dedicated volunteer party groups, the revitalization of the official apparatus, the coming of age of a new generation of leaders in both camps intent on injecting more partisan meaning into California's public affairs, were all harbingers of death for the ultra-nonpartisan era that was Earl Warren's. The state's spiraling and ever-throbbing population, that past scourge of electoral regularity that still lessens it today compared with other jurisdictions, may nevertheless be the instigator of further endeavors to strengthen party fealty. Now the biggest state in the Union, California has found its place in the sun in American politics and its weight lies ever heavier in the electoral college and in the halls of Congress. Many of her outstanding personalities of both Republican and Democratic persuasion have made, and will continue to make, their marks in the country as a whole. Such augmented significance for California can be a mighty influence in molding both state parties into more energetic offshoots of their respective national organizations.

These developments may create a dilemma for Republicans in years to come. The lesson taught by Warren in political strategy may become all the more essential for office seekers running under the Republican banner in California, given the continuing GOP deficit within the electorate. Yet as partisan considerations become more critical in state public life, it will be harder for most candidates and officers, especially the governor, to remain as aloof from such concerns as did Warren. In that sense California will probably never again see an Earl Warren in Sacramento. Yet his fundamental beliefs not only endure but have a magnitudinous impact on the American scene today as they are applied to the great constitutional issues that challenge him and his colleagues on the United States Supreme Court.

CHAPTER VII

Mr. Chief Justice

"Individualism" and "Cooperative Endeavor" in a Judicial Setting

Earl Warren's basic ideology and certain practices he developed and polished while governor of California are reflected in his service as chief justice of the United States. An individualist by conviction and by political tempering in the state, he was also most deferential to the beliefs of others, no matter how divergent from his own. As state chief executive he went to great lengths to seek as many diverse thoughts as possible in fashioning his policies and to give them a cordial and attentive hearing. Likewise, the hallmark of the "Warren court" and of his personal opinions in civil liberties cases has been a diligent protection of the individual against governmental force. A lack of intimacy with specific large interest groups or a political party in his gubernatorial days has permitted an easier identification with the rights of minorities.

Warren came to the high tribunal in October, 1953, through appointment by President Eisenhower. He immediately found himself in the midst of a profound dialogue about the court's role in society, a debate by no means limited to the present day. Leading one side of the argument was the late Felix Frankfurter, brilliant and scholarly former law professor at Harvard and probably the outstanding figure on the bench for many years. His rationale was that jurists should exercise the utmost self-restraint in making decisions and refuse to interject their own ideas into interpretations of the Constitution and acts of other government agencies. Jurists were subject to human frailties, answerable ultimately to nothing but their own consciences, and should try earnestly to defer to the popularly chosen branches of government since public opinion could not touch them as directly as it could Congress or the President— a view expounded years before by Oliver Wendell Holmes.

At the other pole of the dispute stood Hugo Black, former New Deal senator from Alabama and a fighter for social reform who distrusts legal subtleties. In contrast to Frankfurter, Black considers the court to be one of justice more than of law and is a passionate defender of individual freedoms through the energetic exertion of judicial authority against other units of government. Thus, from the moment he donned his robes, the former California governor was destined to become one of history's most influential justices, simply because he would gravitate to one position or the other. He soon joined the Black camp, ardently advocating judicial activism, particularly for personal liberties. The new head man became a member of a bloc composed initially of Black, William O. Douglas, and himself. They have since formed the nucleus of a liberal majority that has more often than not had its way in recent years.

Warren and his colleagues have breathed new life into the Fifth Amendment's guarantee against self-incrimination in federal and state investigatory procedures. A narrow but significant 5-4 ruling came in 1957 in *Watkins v. United States*, written by the Chief Justice.[1] The defendant was a former union official who had declined to answer questions put to him by the House Committee on Un-American Activities. His conviction for contempt of Congress was reversed because the pertinency of the item to which he refused to respond was not made clear to him. Warren went beyond the immediate issue to warn that the power of enquiry had its limits: "There is no general authority to expose the private affairs of individuals just for the sake of revelation. Probes conducted solely for . . . personal aggrandizement . . . or to 'punish' . . . are indefensible."

---

[1] 354 U.S. 178 (1957).

The Chief Justice lectured that "the Bill of Rights is applicable to investigations as to all forms of governmental action. Witnesses cannot be compelled to give evidence against themselves. They cannot be subject to unreasonable search and seizure." He ventured to say that such inquests were encompassed by First Amendment safeguards: "The mere summoning of a witness and compelling him to testify, against his will, about his beliefs, expressions or associations is a measure of governmental interference. And when those forced revelations concern matters that are unorthodox, unpopular, or even hateful to the general public, the reaction in the life of the witness may be disastrous." The situation was even worse if past sentiments and memberships were disclosed and judged by current standards rather than those applicable at that time.

Indeed, it was not only the people called in an investigation who suffered. Those named by them during the proceedings were placed in the same glare of publicity and also held up to "stigma, scorn and obloquy. Beyond that, there is the more subtle and immeasurable effect upon those who tend to adhere to the . . . uncontroversial . . . to avoid a similar fate at some future time." Warren had great respect for the doctrine of separation of powers and especially for the autonomy of lawmakers. Yet that could not take precedence over the preservation of human liberties: "No doubt every reasonable indulgence . . . must be accorded to . . . a coordinate branch. . . . But such deference cannot yield to an unnecessary and unreasonable dissipation of precious constitutional freedoms."

Warren also spoke for the court majority in reversing the verdict for contempt against Professor Paul Sweezy in 1957.[2] The action arose from a state interrogation conducted by New Hampshire's attorney general under the aegis of the legislature. Sweezy had refused to respond to questions asked him regarding a lecture he had delivered at the state university and his relationship to the Progressive party and the Progressive Citizens of America. The Chief Justice invoked the First Amendment

---

[2] *Sweezy v. New Hampshire,* 354 U.S. 234 (1957).

through the Fourteenth and asserted that "there unquestionably was an invasion of petitioner's liberties in the areas of academic freedom and . . . expression—areas in which the government should be extremely reticent to tread."

Political self-determination for each person is an equally fundamental tenet in this country, said Warren: "Exercise of these basic freedoms . . . has traditionally been through the media of political association. Any interference with the freedom of party is simultaneously an interference with the freedom of its adherents." He put his own nonpartisan bent in a new light when he observed that "all political ideas cannot and should not be channeled into the programs of our two major parties. History has amply proved the virtue of . . . activity by minority, dissident groups, who innumerable times have been in the vanguard of democratic thought and whose programs were ultimately accepted. Mere unorthodoxy or dissent from the prevailing mores is not to be condemned. The absence of such voices would be a symptom of grave illness in our society."

Warren's devotion to the maximum shielding of individual belief and affiliation, no matter how deviant, was evident in the litigation aimed at Communists and subversion control. In 1956 he held that Pennsylvania card-carrier Steve Nelson could not be prosecuted under that state's statutes for conspiring to encourage the forcible overthrow of the *federal* government. The Chief Justice said Congress had intended to pre-empt the whole province of anti-subversive legislation and supercede all similar state laws through the 1940 Smith Act. He voted with most of his colleagues the following year in *Yates v. United States* to clear fourteen Communists of his native California. The tribunal concluded that the Smith Act did not forbid "advocacy and teaching" of the violent destruction of the national government as an abstract principle; there had to be inducement to action. In 1965 the Chief Executive and his associates rendered ineffective the law requiring the Communist party and other subversive organizations to register.

That same year Warren confirmed that a Communist could hold union office, nullifying a section of the 1959 Landrum-

Griffin Act.[3] He was persuaded that the relevant stipulation was a bill of attainder, a legislative enactment inflicting retribution without legal trial. Here, indeed, was a far-reaching attempt to guard against governmental invasion of private prerogatives. Even if the lawmakers could logically conclude that some card-carriers would use their positions to induce political strikes, they could not assume automatically that all party members shared these evil purposes. The Chief Justice remarked: "We do not hold today that Congress cannot weed dangerous persons out of the labor movement. . . . Rather, we make again the point . . . that Congress must accomplish such results by rules of general applicability. It cannot specify the people upon whom the sanction it prescribes is to be levied." Ironically, the man freed was Archie Brown, a San Francisco longshoreman, who had contested Warren for the California statehouse in 1946 after the Governor had taken both Republican and Democratic nominations in the June primaries.

The Chief Justice's words from a 1962 article are testimony to his position on civil liberties: "I am one who believes firmly that the court must be vigilant against neglect . . . of our Bill of Rights. . . . Legislative or executive action . . . in the name of security cannot be placed on a scale that weighs the public's interest against that of the individual in a sort of 'count the heads' fashion. Democracy under our Constitution calls for judicial deference to the coordinate branches of the government and their judgment of what is essential to the protection of the nation. But it calls no less for a steadfast protection of those fundamentals imbedded in the Constitution, so incorporated for the express purpose of insulating them from possible excesses of the moment."[4]

The Supreme Court's presiding officer cast his lot with a majority of his associates in a number of other libertarian edicts, giving wide scope to human freedoms. They decreed that when

---

[3] *United States v. Brown*, 381 U.S. 437 (1965).

[4] Earl Warren, "The Bill of Rights and the Military," *New York University Law Review*, 37, No. 2 (Apr., 1962), 201-2. (From the James Madison Lecture given at New York Univ. Law Center.) © New York Univ.

a poor person is charged with a felony and cannot afford an attorney, the state must furnish him one without cost. Furthermore, the accused must not only be allowed to consult with counsel when initially detained by the police, he must be so informed by the authorities and told also of his right to remain silent. The tribunal reversed precedents established decades ago to ordain that the Fifth Amendment's wording against self-incrimination applies to both state and federal proceedings. The constitutional injunction against illegal search and seizure was made binding on evidence presented in state and federal trials.

An experienced prosecuting attorney, Warren is dedicated to fair and orderly hearings. This is why he feels that television and live photography have no place in courtroom sessions. It was largely at his urging that in 1962 the judicial conference resolved that under no circumstances would there be pictures or broadcasts in federal tribunals. Indeed, in 1965 the Supreme Court threw out the swindling conviction of Texas financier Billie Sol Estes (though not other counts) on grounds that televising portions of his testimony over his objections deprived him of due process under the Fourteenth Amendment.

That the Chief Justice was willing to turn every stone searching for a means to shelter the individual from official pressure was dramatically demonstrated in the 1958 case of Albert Trop.[5] Trop's passport application was denied because under the Nationality Act of 1940, he supposedly lost his citizenship as a result of a court-martial and dishonorable discharge from the Army for wartime desertion. Warren opined that the government could not divest citizenship and, uniquely, that the Eighth Amendment's prohibition of cruel and unusual punishment did not permit it. While there was no physical mistreatment or torture here, it was a penalty even more primitive than that because it destroyed the person's very status in organized society. An expatriate had "lost the right to have rights. . . . He may be subject to banishment, a fate universally decried by civilized people. He is stateless, a condition deplored in the international community of democracies. It is no answer to suggest that all

---

[5] *Trop v. Dulles*, 356 U.S. 86 (1958).

the disastrous consequences . . . may not be brought to bear on a . . . person. The threat makes the punishment obnoxious."

Still another interesting facet of Warren's reverence for the individual is evident in his statements and actions on reapportionment. In 1962 he backed the majority in *Baker v. Carr,* holding that the judiciary can and should take jurisdiction in instances of alleged legislative maldistricting to correct any obvious violation of equal protection of the laws under the Fourteenth Amendment. In 1964 the court spelled out further the meaning of its *Baker* findings by requiring the states to strive for popular balance in drawing up constituencies for the House of Representatives. Yet the most eventful, indeed earth-shaking, decision came that same year in *Reynolds v. Sims,*[6] when the population standard was stretched to embrace both chambers of state legislatures. The Chief Justice himself drafted the court's official opinion, averring that "the right to vote freely for the candidate of one's choice is of the essence of a democratic society, and any restrictions . . . strike at the heart of representative government." It was his thesis that the fundamental freedom of the franchise could be as effectively eliminated by diluting the weight of a person's ballot as by completely withholding it. He referred to the conclusion the nation's highest bench had reached in 1963 in *Gray v. Sanders,* sounding the death knell for Georgia's county unit system: " 'The conception of political equality from the Declaration of Independence, to Lincoln's Gettysburg Address, to the Fifteenth, Seventeenth, and Nineteenth Amendments can mean only one thing—one person, one vote.' " The suffrage is personal in nature and touches a sensitive area of human liberty, because the prerogative of an unimpaired voice in the polling undergirds all elemental civil and political rights.

Warren pointed out in *Reynolds* that "legislators represent people, not trees or acres. Legislators are elected by voters, not farms or cities or economic interests." To him, "a citizen . . . is not more nor no less so because he lives in the city or on the farm. . . ." In fact, this was at the core of "Lincoln's vision of 'government of the people, by the people, and for the people.' "

[6] 377 U.S. 533 (1964).

The Chief Justice felt that acquiescence to minority dominance would abrogate the majority's will "in a way that far surpassed any possible denial of minority rights that might otherwise be thought to result." The American system provided ample sanctuary to minorities by means other than giving them sway over state legislatures. The Fourteenth Amendment demanded no less than substantially equal representation in both chambers for all men and women, regardless of "place" or "race." The former California governor who had once defended the "federal analogy" for his own senate now saw it as irrelevant.

Warren's obeisance to cooperation and collaboration, a preoccupation in labor affairs when he was in Sacramento, stayed with him after he went to Washington and found its way into union-management litigation. In such matters he is known as a pre-emptionist, one inclined to emphasize Washington's primacy at the expense of the states. Although this might seem strange for one who as governor so frequently stressed and practiced a viable states'-rights policy, there is reason for it. Besides the fact that he now views the field from a loftier berth, he is convinced that uniformity in collective bargaining rules is the surest way to peaceful worker-employer dealings.

The Chief Justice took an extraordinary step in 1957 to implement this faith. That year his majority declaration in *Guss v. Utah Labor Relations Board* created a no-man's land in terms of federal-state jurisdiction in collective-bargaining cases, a condition that Congress had to rectify through the 1959 Landrum-Griffin Act. The vacuum might have been filled by permitting the N.L.R.B. sufficient flexibility to extend its coverage in certain instances or by allowing industries and single companies to come under national fiat when their business volume exceeded a certain percentage. Yet the outcome might be new findings of illegality under the higher authority on matters previously legitimate under the state, something that might lead to disruptive squabbles between labor and management. Collective bargaining should be carried on in a sympathetic and agreeable atmosphere, and the tribunal should have no part in fostering friction or bitterness.

The Judicial Administrator: Pragmatic "Problem Solving" and "Cooperative Endeavor" on the Supreme Court

Warren's practicality motivated him to seek a smooth-functioning administration when he sat in the statehouse at Sacramento. The same has been true of his service in Washington, and he wasted little time setting the judicial house in order. The chief justiceship is largely what its holder makes of it, entailing few formal duties except the normal functions of any magistrate on the top bench. The Constitution makes no special provision for the post, simply indicating that the high court shall be composed of a chief and several associate justices and directing the chief to oversee impeachment proceedings in the senate against the President. Besides that assignment and a slightly bigger salary, his position in the tribunal's decision-making process is not legally superior to that of his colleagues. Nonetheless, he has several managerial responsibilities which influence the operations and spirit not only of the Supreme Court but of the entire federal judiciary.

First, he presides over the body of nine men in open hearings and in closed-door conferences and has the privilege of commenting on business at hand before the other members. Warren's clerks make memos on each application to be heard, and he then reviews their notes and official documents. Armed with a few personal summaries of these items, he outlines the problem and makes recommendations to his colleagues—always stressing the practical as well as legal consequences of any matter. One scholar, who thinks the former California governor has brought the most authority to the chief justiceship since Charles Evans Hughes, tells us that the chief's function in this respect is like that of a leader striking the pitch for the orchestra: his example can set the tone of the entire session.[7] Warren has been a skilled,

---

[7] Bernard Schwartz, " 'Warren Court'—An Opinion," *New York Times Magazine*, June 30, 1957, 10.

businesslike moderator from the outset. His predecsssor, Fred Vinson, was generally unsuccessful at settling quarrels and Harlan Fiske Stone before him tended to allow debate to run on interminably. On the other hand, Warren tries to keep conversation on track. He holds himself to a few brief remarks and then allots several well-timed minutes to each of the others, traditionally in order of seniority. His benign bearing has brought an atmosphere of harmony to these meetings. Before Warren assumed the position, and particularly under Vinson, the nation's principal bench was torn by discord, frequently in full public view. Sharp philosophic divisions still endure; blocs of "activists" versus "restrainers" and of "liberals" versus "conservatives" still exist, as they have throughout history. Yet these differences are no longer exacerbated by personal antagonisms to the degree they once were, and the court has thus been able to speak with more consistency. Perhaps the high point of Warren's stewardship in this regard was reached in his first major ruling, the 1954 school desegregation case. It was no mean accomplishment for the court's neophyte to induce eight, often wrangling, individualists, never hesitant to articulate their convictions, to join in a unanimous decison.

The Chief Justice also assigns the writing of opinions. His use of this power will influence both the evolution of the law and his own relations with his colleagues. Determined to be the leader in fact as well as title, Warren has often reserved for himself the most controversial litigation on which to expound. His deep sense of personal accountability has led him frequently to serve as a lightning rod, absorbing much of the criticism that might have been hurled with greater fervor and more validity at some of his associates.

Warren prepares his own judicial opinions, whether in majority or dissent, with the same meticulousness and penchant for the facts as he did in developing his programs in Sacramento. He first dictates a memorandum for each dispute. He then reviews it and the original briefs with one of his clerks before studying them extensively on his own, a procedure reminiscent of his handling of departmental reports prior to meetings of the Governor's Council. All official hearings are recorded and these he usually plays back several times. His assistant then prepares a second draft based on their exchanges and the basic material; together they rephrase it as often as necessary. When the final narrative is almost ready for release, the Chief Justice regularly replays the oral argument in search of that one last important detail.

Warren also has executive tasks pertaining to the whole federal judicial structure. With the gusto of a dedicated administrator, he has taken upon himself the obligation of supervising the entire system. In past decades overseeing the courts around the country belonged to no one in particular. Each local jurist was lord of his own domain and central guidance was unknown. William Howard Taft was instrumental in securing a 1922 act establishing a Judicial Conference of the United States, a gathering of senior national appellate judges from each major region under the chairmanship of the chief justice. In time the institution deteriorated into a club for elderly gentlemen. It remained for Warren to make it viable once again. When he went to Washington, its members averaged about eighty years of age. Quietly but diligently he saw to it that when a man reached seventy he would no longer be in charge of his circuit nor represent it at the capital. That done, he next included the trial judges for the first time in the organization's existence. Prior to Warren's tenure, the chief justice himself was merely a non-voting gavel rapper at the parley. Warren wasted no time in changing that situation also.

Warren has energized the Conference in many ways. He makes every effort to have all legislation concerning the federal judiciary either originate with his group or be referred to it for scrutiny, a move similar to his use of experts on various advisory bodies in clearing his programs in California. Regulations for all national tribunals are now basically within the province of the conference. The Chief Justice quickly took command of the administrative office of the courts by hand-picking a well-qualified director and assistant and closely superintending their operations. If one section of the country now falls behind in its work because of a sudden burst of new litigation or because someone takes ill, the office assigns other jurists to help ease the burden. Annual statistical tabulations, the facts on case loads, dispensations, and other items permit the Chief and all others in the hierarchy to ascertain their branch's over-all performance. These enumerations are also spurs to efficiency.

Warren has endeavored to improve the judicial machinery through the rule-making authority that lies formally with the Supreme Court. Those stipulations cover an array of points and minutiae, such as who can be included in a lawsuit, what questions each side may put to the other before trial, and how some things are to be presented to the judge or jury. In the late forties activity here had ground to a near halt. Exploring ways of rejuvenating the process, the Chief Justice emulated his days in Sacramento by appointing six committees to pursue the matter. He still selects personally the membership of these units from lawyers, magistrates, and law professors around the country who collectively constitute a cross section of the legal profession. Warren meets for a time with each group and closely inspects its undertakings, again reminiscent of his activities as governor. Their communiqués then go to the Conferences, to the high tribunal, and finally to Congress. Warren guides their progress every step of the way.

The Chief Justice's grip on the whole judicial mechanism is shown also by his avid participation in the American Law Institute, an organization of some fifteen hundred lawyers and jurists from across the land. They gather yearly in Washington to dissect legal issues salient to both federal and state courts. Warren regularly and eagerly attends these colloquies and renders a report of his own on a variety of topics, from improving probation arrangements to decreasing the cost of bankruptcy pleadings. Frank tells us that in listening to him one realizes that the legal system in this country is not merely a headless juggernaut, that there is someone at the helm who actually knows what is going on from coast to coast and is desirous of making it better.[8] Thus Warren is probably our first real chief justice of the United States and not simply the presiding officer of the top bench.

Warren's pragmatic demeanor and obsession for thorough familiarity with the facts are also mirrored in many of his written opinions. They are ordinarily brief compared to the lengthy, digressive, and technical pronouncements of some jurists, and constructed with clear and concise phraseology understandable to the average layman. A dedication to an unobstructed examination of ideas was obvious in his words in the *Sweezy* appeal (*supra*): "To impose any straitjacket upon the intellectual leaders of our colleges and universities would imperil the future of our nation. No field of education is so thoroughly comprehended by man that new discoveries cannot yet be made. Particularly is this true in the social sciences, where few, if any, principles are accepted as absolutes. Scholarship cannot flourish in an atmosphere of suspicion and distrust. Teachers and students must always remain free to inquire, to study and to evaluate, to gain new maturity and understanding; otherwise our civilization will stagnate and die."

In the labor field the Chief Justice is not disposed to legalistic distinctions that fall short of practical meaning. Exemplary was his 1958 dissent in *International Association of Machinists v. Gonzales*: "The presence or absence of pre-emption [by the federal government over the states] is . . . not a game that is played with labels or an exercise in artful pleading."[9] He joined Justice Douglas in disagreeing with another judgment the same year, refusing to go along with the technicalities invoked by the majority: "The present decision is capricious. The boycott is lawful if the employer agrees to abide by this collective bargaining agreement. It is unlawful if the employer reneges."[10] Two

---

[8] John P. Frank, *The Warren Court* (New York: Macmillan, 1964), p. 23.

[9] 356 U.S. 617 (1958).

[10] *Local 1976, Carpenters v. N.L.R.B.*, 357 U.S. 93 (1958).

authorities maintain that Warren's reasoning in this realm does not exceed the requirements of the question. He does not use a case as a vehicle for establishing a broader policy or for dwelling on constitutional issues not raised by the facts.[11]

The above contention has not always been true, particularly when human liberties are involved. In this area the Chief Justice has often tended to educate the public, to sermonize beyond the purely legal point at stake. This has been induced partly by his penchant for addressing himself to all possible implications of a matter and conscientiously reporting to his "constituents." In the *Watkins* case (*supra*) his essential finding was that the scope of a congressional committee's authority must be firmly clarified by the resolution setting it up and a witness must be shown plainly the relevance of questions asked. However, Warren refused to stop with that and seized the occasion to read an essay upon abuse of the investigatory prerogative and its relation to various constitutional provisions, all of which was unnecessary to the court's narrow ruling. With time his decisions even in this category have lost some of their sweeping quality and taken on a more analytic polish. Still, the apparently irrepressible urge to lecture the American people has never been completely contained.

Judicial Activism, the Individual, and Constitutional Fundamentals

Warren was an ardent fan of separation of powers when he occupied California's executive mansion. Yet he came to Washington from a job that had immersed him in pressing daily concerns and accustomed him to problem solving, the influence of his personality and character aside. Small wonder that he manifested this trait on the bench as well. He quickly became an activist habituated to asserting the powers of the court rela-

---

[11] Sam Kagel and Virginia Smith, "Chief Justice Warren and Labor Law," *California Law Review*, 49, No. 1 (Mar., 1961), 142.

tive to other arms and agencies of government, especially when they were pitted against the individual. In the *Trop* litigation (*supra*), one of those rare instances where a federal law was nullified, the Chief Justice was mindful of the independence of the branches. Nevertheless, that cardinal tenet could not stand in the way of full protection of personal freedoms. He noted that while the judiciary should not delve into the wisdom of legislative enactments, neither could it sanction what was constitutionally proscribed. Its duty was to implement the basic document's safeguards of individual rights.

In *Trop*, Warren observed that "the provisions of the Constitution are not timeworn adages or hollow shibboleths. They are vital, living principles that authorize and limit governmental powers in our nation. . . . When it appears that an act of congress conflicts with one of these provisions, we have no choice but to enforce the paramount commands of the Constitution. We are sworn to do no less. . . . We do well to approach this task cautiously, as all our predecesssors have counseled. But the ordeal of judgment cannot be shirked. In some eighty-one instances since this court was established it has determined that congressional action exceeded the bounds of the Constitution. It is so in this case."[12]

Again in *Watkins*, circumscription of the national lawmakers' investigatory function was invoked with ardent and comprehensive language. There and in other verdicts Warren also saw his responsibility as the preventing of one official sector from overstepping itself relative to the others. A mandate to conduct inquests must not be confused with law enforcement, for the latter belongs properly to the executive and judiciary. However misguided or extreme in its specific applications, here was a belief grounded on respect for the division of powers. In the *Sweezy* case Warren held that the legislature had not allowed New Hampshire's attorney general to obtain the information he attempted to elicit from the professor; therefore the state executive officer had exceeded his jurisdiction.

---

[12] *Trop v. Dulles*, pp. 103-4.

In labor hearings the Chief Justice's support for federal pre-emption is explained partly by his observance of the doctrines of separation and federalism. If something is within the national Congress' orbit, then it is not for the magistrates to act in its place—in the *Guss* case (*supra*)—by strengthening the states' hands in collective bargaining. In that litigation Warren spoke in favor of a no-man's land rather than upsetting the supremacy of the House and Senate. When a delegation to an agency (N.L.R.B.) has been made by the legislators, it was not for the tribunal to usurp it. Effective government could be achieved only within well-defined areas of authority. In these and certain other suits Warren did not conform to the activist mold he has cast for himself generally over the years.

Yet in most civil liberties appeals he reverted to type, pulling a tight rein on the executive in Washington in several edicts that he wrote directly or to which he assented. In the aftermath of the *Yates* decree in 1957 (*supra*) the Justice Department found itself unable to obtain guilty verdicts under the Smith Act and consented to dismissal of many pending prosecutions. In the *Jencks* case the same year, that agency was ordered to permit criminal defendants to inspect certain records. Warren and his colleagues affirmed in 1958 that the Secretary of State had committed a transgression against the passport laws in refusing citizens permission to leave the country because of their political beliefs and associations. Indeed, the Secretary was told that he had not followed his own prescribed procedures on discharge of employees for disloyalty. Consequently, one John Service was reinstated to the foreign service in 1957 after a six-year fight. Even the military felt the restraining hand of the high court. In the 1955 *Toth* action the court not only stopped military trials of civilians but voided a federal statute authorizing such proceedings after release from the armed forces for crimes committed while still in uniform. The Army was informed in 1958 that it could not give a soldier a less than honorable discharge because of alleged subversive activities that took place before his induction.

In California's governorship Warren was a devotee of states' rights—in a positive sense. Lower-level officials should exert themselves to the utmost to resolve as many public issues as feasible, turning to Washington only as a last resort. Nevertheless, he was also dedicated to a meaningful concept of federalism. That which belongs logically and appropriately under national jurisdiction should, in his view, lie completely with its agencies. In defending indivdual rights through national endeavor, Warren has put the judicial machinery to unsparing use in curbing *state* laws and activities when the facts and the axioms of the Constitution seem to dictate. In the 1956 *Pennsylvania vs. Nelson* litigation the Chief Justice argued that Congress meant to reserve subversion control to itself and to supersede all corresponding state laws through the 1940 Smith Act. Nor could the states decline to admit applicants to the bar because of questionable allegiance, he and his colleagues ruled the following year. In 1964 Warren stood with the majority as it struck down a Washington state requirement that all public employees take a loyalty oath. Lately in criminal proceedings he and most of his colleagues have directed the states to furnish attorneys to indigent people, to inform suspects of their rights to attorneys and to remain silent when being queried by the police, to apply the constitutional deterrent to self-incrimination to their proceedings, and to invoke the same guarantees against unreasonable search and seizure as do our federal courts.

Warren's notion that the judiciary must plunge itself thoroughly and zealously into the problems facing Americans was dramatically emphasized on the topic of legislative reapportionment. Here again was a vigorous exertion by the tribunal in instructing the states to resolve issues they had failed to dispose of on their own. His sentiments in the *Baker* and *Wesberry* decisions (*supra*) and his 1964 expressions in *Reynolds v. Sims* (*supra*) were a far cry from the Vinson court's ruling in 1946 in *Colegrove v. Green*. There the justices refused to set aside an apportionment law that had created congressional districts of pronounced unevenness. They claimed then that the question of representation was "political" rather than judicial and thus not proper for the court's scrutiny. It was up to the solons, partic-

ularly in the states, to eliminate any rotten borough. Nevertheless, the passage of time demonstrated their unwillingness or
inability, or both, to correct such wrongdoings. Warren and his
associates felt they must intervene to fulfill an obligation
abandoned by those to whom it had initially been given.

In his historic finding in *Reynolds*, Warren informed the
states that everyone was entitled to full and effective participation in his state's legislative operations. This necessitated substantial equality in the election of its members: "Modern and
viable state government needs, and the Constitution demands,
no less." The Chief Justice exposed his readiness to use his
position to tackle any practical obstacles that might emasculate
personal freedoms when he observed: "We are told that the
matter of apportioning representation . . . is a complex and
many-faceted one. . . . We are cautioned about the dangers of
entering into political thickets and mathematical quagmires:
Our answer is this: a denial of constitutionally protected rights
demands judicial protection; our oath and our office require no
less of us."[13] He rejected the applicability of the "federal
analogy" to state second chambers with a "common-sense" account of American history. The realities of that day simply
demanded a compromise between the larger and the smaller
states in setting up the new Congress to avert a deadlock in the
constitutional convention.

Warren provided practical guidelines for the states in meeting the *Reynolds* judgment. The edict did not mean that there
could be absolutely no distinction in the composition and complexion of the two bodies. Different constituencies might be
established, perhaps based on varying single and multi-member
districts. The lengths of terms did not have to be the same, nor
did the sizes of the two houses or the geographical expanse and
coverage of districts. He and his fellow jurists intended by their
judgment only that the states make efforts, "honest and in good
faith," to construct voting units as nearly even in population as
feasible: "We realize that it is a practical impossibility to arrange
legislative districts so that each one has an identical number of

---

13 *Reynolds v. Sims*, 377 U.S. 533 (1964) pp. 565-66.

residents. . . . Mathematical exactness . . . is hardly a workable constitutional requirement."[14]

The Chief Justice showed his pliability in *Reynolds* by leaving it to inferior tribunals to supervise the ensuing procedures in *ad hoc* fashion, as he did in the school desegregation question. They would work out more concrete standards in the context of actual litigation, since it was not expedient for Washington to specify any precise tests for the present. What was marginally permissible in one state might be unsatisfactory in another, depending on circumstances. Developing a body of doctrine on a case-by-case basis was the best method of resolving the matter. Warren even had some useful advice for the subordinate judges, indicating that their remedies in such a new venture would of course have to adjust to a "variety of local conditions." When an election is pending and the machinery is already in motion, "equitable considerations might justify . . . withholding . . . immediately effective relief. . . . A court can reasonably endeavor to avoid a disruption . . . which might result from requiring precipitate changes that could make unreasonable or embarrassing demands. . . ."[15]

Social Progress, Adaptability, and Judicial Activism: The Race Issue

The most signal accomplishment of the high tribunal under Warren and the one that brought him the most personal attention was *Brown v. Board of Education* in 1954. The Chief Justice himself wrote the unanimous opinion.[16] The absence of dissent was a remarkable achievement testifying to his talents as a unifier, and an invaluable symbol to the entire country. It probably would have been impossible under the divisive Vinson court. This stroke, perhaps more than any other, manifested Warren's perseverance in the cause of social progress, his adaptability,

[14] *Ibid.*, p. 577.
[15] *Ibid.*, p. 585.
[16] 347 U.S. 483 (1954).

and his proneness to judicial activism. He denied that a meaningful assessment of the repercussions of segregation could be based merely on tangible factors, holding that to isolate children "from others of similar age and qualifications solely because of their race generates a feeling of inferiority as to their status in the community that may affect their hearts and minds in a way unlikely ever to be undone."

Overturning the 1896 *Plessy v. Ferguson* ruling of the top bench that had approved exclusive arrangements in transportation for Negroes and Whites if substantially equivalent in a material sense, the Chief Justice concluded "that in the field of public education the doctrine of 'separate but equal' has no place. Separate . . . facilities are inherently unequal." Far-reaching as it was, Warren's reflexive moderation and pragmatism intruded into the implementation of his historic dictum. A host of regional complexities compelled him and his colleagues to hear further arguments from interested parties regarding methods of securing compliance. The Chief Justice sought a pivotal role for the localities by placing the prime responsibility for action on the school boards. The federal district judges were instructed to oversee and appraise these moves because of their proximity to existing difficulties, in much the same manner as later on reapportionment. In shaping their remedies the courts were to obey equitable principles, which had long been characterized by "practical flexibility." Warren permitted the lower tribunals to determine whether the defendants had made a prompt and reasonable start toward conformity. He spelled out what the judges might wish to consider in supervising the process "with all deliberate speed."

The *Brown* finding had been foreshadowed by the judicial invalidation of segregation in universities under Vinson. Furthermore, the 1954 decision seemed at first not to encounter much opposition on the surface. However, it apparently took a little time for the shock to wear off. When it did, the reaction was vigorous and even bitter in some quarters. Renewed outbreaks of violence, the formation of "white citizens' councils" to seek techniques (ostensibly proper but frequently stimulating those of oppressive character) to frustrate the edict, and the passage of state statutes assenting to abolition of regular primary and secondary institutions or to the cutoff of tax monies from those that integrated, were all features of the wake of this landmark pronouncement. Direct challenges to it were made by physically barring Negro youngsters from admittance to schools. The most ostentatious event of that kind took place in the fall of 1957 at Little Rock, Arkansas, when Governor Orval Faubus sent state police to keep Negro children out of Central High. President Eisenhower dispatched troops to prevent meddling with the execution of a federal court directive. In *Cooper v. Aaron* in 1958, Warren and his colleagues unanimously sustained the lower tribunal in Arkansas. Their opinion was signed separately by each member, showing that despite the turnover on the Supreme Court since 1954, all agreed with the earlier mandate and were committed to its effectuation.

The Chief Justice and his fellows have consistently tried to preserve the integrity of their original desegration order. It is to their great credit that they have been able to stand as one for over a decade, with no significant schisms on this and related questions. Integration would surely have been far more troublesome and costly if the nine men had not unswervingly held the line, a leadership *tour de force* attributable in no small way to Warren himself. In *Cooper* they warned the most diehard southerners that there would be no retreat in the face of massive, even bellicose, resistance. In other litigation since then they have stressed that no undue procrastination will be tolerated.

In other appeals the nation's high court carried the new dogma on race relations from academic pursuits to all state operations. In still others it gave broad scope to the word *state* in the Fourteenth Amendment, preventing such evasions as the leasing of official classrooms to private parties or abolishing the public system entirely and paying for tuition of boys and girls to enroll elsewhere. Warren and his associates used their school ruling as a springboard to buttress Negro rights in other substantive fields. In *Heart of Atlanta Motel v. United States* in 1964, they insisted that the public accommodations section of the civil rights act of that year was constitutional, based on Congress' power to regulate interstate commerce. The 1954 injunction and its extention to other provinces, and the retaliation it triggered below the Mason-Dixon Line, helped launch a mounting civil rights campaign—a rising level of hope, expectations and agitation by American Negroes. Certainly it pricked the national conscience and led to further pursuits to remove once and for all our primary domestic disgrace and international embarrassment. The federal civil rights laws of 1957, 1960, 1964, and 1965 on this subject are monuments partly to the tribunal's intervention.

Here was another illustration of Warren's predisposition to enter the breach actively to rectify a shortcoming on which others had reneged. The Supreme Court stepped into a vacuum left by the default of the national lawmakers and of the executive. Each of the three post-Civil War amendments of the Constitution designed to ensure fair treatment for the Negro—the Thirteenth, Fourteenth, and Fifteenth—apparently placed with the House and the Senate the primary mission of according redress "through appropriate legislation." A spate of statutes in the Reconstruction period was largely demolished by the court. After 1875 and until the late 1950's the solons shirked their duty of consummating those constitutional safeguards—procrastination which ultimately brought on compensations by the other two branches.

The judiciary has generally surpassed Congress and the administration in aggressive performance in civil rights protection under the incumbent chief justice, although recent efforts by the national legislature and the White House have again brought them resolutely into the picture. Yet there is no gainsaying that judicial declarations, led in the main by Earl Warren, not only shook the states out of their listlessness but propelled the other arms of the federal government to new heights of exertion. Possibly there is a form of belated justice here, for it was the court of an earlier epoch, particularly in the late nineteenth century by erecting hindrances like *Plessy*, that must take most of the blame for neutralizing the Fourteenth Amendment and the legal stipulations aimed at realizing it. Indeed, the tribunal frustrated the very purpose for which the war between the states was fought. If the life of that constitutional guarantee was originally taken by the Supreme Court, a new one was given it under Warren.

The Chief Justice and His Critics

The general tenor of the verdicts handed down by the Chief Justice and his associates have brought down upon their heads a torrent of criticism. For their findings in the realm of race relations they have been vilified. The more fanatical question the jurists' collective sanity and liken them to history's better-known tyrants. The allegation of sympathy for communism is mild compared to some other charges. More restrained, but no less serious, are accusations that the Supreme Court has thrown precedent out the window in overturning *Plessy*, that it has destroyed our federal system by binding and gagging states' rights, and, with more validity, that it came to its conclusions in *Brown*, not on law but by way of sociological and psychological considerations. These and similar indictments, notably a complaint of sabotaging the separation-of-powers doctrine, have been hurled from a myriad of sources on other topics.

Certainly the rulings that deal with religion have added fuel to the fire. In *Engel v. Vitale* in 1962 the high court knocked out, as contrary to the First Amendment on separation of church and state, the daily recitation of a so-called nondenominational prayer in some New York classrooms. Another judgment vowed that nonbelievers in God could not be excluded from holding public office. Protests came in loud and clear from such spiritual leaders as Cardinal Spellman and other Catholic clergy, Billy Graham, and some Fundamentalist spokesmen. Many in military and patriotic circles were angered when in 1965 the high bench told conscientious objectors that it was unnecessary to have faith in a Supreme Being to escape military service. One need only have a "sincere and meaningful belief" which occupies in his life the same place that God does in the lives of others. Warren sided with the majority in each of these instances. A proposed constitutional change to upset the justices' proclamations on worship in the schools has not seen the legal light of day. The policy committee of Warren's own Republican party in the national House of Representatives has adopted the measure as a formal position.

Groups like the American Legion, the Veterans of Foreign Wars, and Daughters of the American Revolution have done the most fretting over the matters of loyalty-security versus free speech and association. The John Birch Society has been driven to frenzied vituperation. Its venture to remove Warren from office is well known. The main body of its indictment centers on the Chief Justice's supposed radicalism, although it covers scores of other imputed high crimes and misdemeanors. Birch-sponsored billboards have appeared urging his ouster, and do-it-yourself impeachment kits are peddled for a nominal sum. Always inventive, these guardians of the American way ran in 1962 an essay contest on "Why Earl Warren Should Be Impeached." The Chief Justice proposed his wife as a contestant: "She knows more about my faults than anyone else."[17] Warren doubtless had the Birchers in mind, along with others of that stripe, when in his eulogy to the assassinated President Kennedy he declared that "such acts are commonly stimulated by forces of hatred and malevolence, such as today are eating their way into the bloodstream of American life."[18]

Much less impassioned and far more respected critics have raised cries of displeasure with the Warren court. Even many presiding magistrates of state supreme courts and several pillars of the American Bar Association have joined the assault. Warren resigned from the A.B.A. in a fit of pique over his admonishment about the trend of judical thinking in Washington. The Council of State Governments has advocated a modification of the Constitution to inaugurate a new Court of the Union, consisting of the chief justices of each of the fifty states. This body could set aside by majority vote any proclamation handed down by the

---

17 "The Warren Court: Fateful Decade," *Newsweek*, LXIII, No. 19 (May 11, 1964), 25.

18 Quoted in Frank, *op. cit.*, p. 36.

nine men in the nation's capital which it deemed to infringe on states' rights. This enterprise remains in limbo thus far. However, bills have been introduced in virtually every session of Congress to contract the jurisdiction of the top bench or nullify its various findings.

The high tribunal has its vindicators, of course. Notable among these are the law faculties of Harvard and Yale, the American Civil Liberties Union, the American Jewish Congress, the New York City bar, and some elements of the American Bar Association. A spirited polemic continues in and beyond legal circles over the scope, methods, and tenor of the Warren court's decisions. Ironically, for the first time in history the reprimands and calumny emanate mainly from the right, the kudos and acclaim from the left. This is a reversal for the detractors and admirers from their earlier stands, before the judiciary's 1937 switch from guardian angel of property to leading custodian of personal freedoms.

Those who disparage the Supreme Court today might well ponder the matter of consistency. They might remember that Warren and his associates have been most conspicious for curbing governmental encroachment on the liberties of private, individual citizens, presumably a cherished cornerstone of their conservative credo. However, the point about consistency might likewise be contemplated by the present tribunal and its laudators as well. Carried to excess, judicial activism (here in the name of libertarianism) can lead to an absolute suzerainty over the other branches. Once again the men on our highest bench could become unchecked censors of the lawmakers and the White House, a role renounced by their predecessors under the whiplash of F.D.R.'s "court-packing" plan. They made a quick transition then to more restraint, scuttling the President's scheme and preserving their independence and integrity in the process. No little ill will had been generated up to that time by the raising of the justices' own notions to a pedestal of constitutional sanctity that nullified statutes desired by many but anathema to them.

Such judicial action occurred in the economic field in the thirties and before, since it was there that the jurists' preconceptions were disturbed. Today, deference to the legislature and executive jibes with the personal convictions of the current justices in that area. The same does not hold true in the realm of human rights, where congressional and other strictures run counter to their beliefs. Nevertheless, it is questionable whether the present incumbents on the Supreme Court are any more entitled than were their pre-1937 forebears to exalt their own views to the degree they seem to do in many instances. Thus another vulnerability of Warren and his colleagues is their sometime impatience to indulge their progressive persuasion in overriding even necessary restrictions of individual rights. Complainants insist that the court is overly doctrinaire and too eager to set straight what it considers amiss. They charge that it is excessively taken with grand abstractions of liberty to the neglect of orderly growth and continuity in the law. It is, in short, unaware of its limitations as an institution. Legalities aside, such tendencies can undermine public confidence and damage the tribunal's effectiveness within the governmental structure. Felix Frankfurter, with his usual testiness, occasionally preached to his brethren on the proper bounds of judicial power, sometimes precipitating heated exchanges with Warren.

Nonetheless, those who commend the Chief Justice and his fellow jurists observe that the judiciary's bedrock function is to construe the Constitution. That document has sweeping and flexible language which invites many possible interpretations and the injection into the decision-making process of personal predilection. In fact, throughout our history all men who have sat on the bench in Washington have tried to define that noble charter in keeping with the times. Each has had to walk a tightrope between revered tradition and inexorable social change. Whether they have attained that delicate balance is a subjective evaluation of contemporary society, as it has always been.

Praise for the Warren court's activism might also be rationalized from a more practical angle. Our nation has burgeoned to such size and complexity that we can no longer resolve our socio-economic and political issues through orthodox channels. Congress is often subjected to so many intense pressures from all sides that it becomes veritably paralyzed. The President must frequently walk with caution, thanks to the rituals of politics. Only the Supreme Court, further removed from the clashing ambitions and passions of the moment, can act in many situations. Indeed, it is doing so under Warren, in the face of lethargy elsewhere, in mending the decades of inequities inflicted upon the Negro, in shielding the individual from arbitrariness by the national lawmakers or states, and in giving the city dweller his due in legislative representation.

A 1955 article by the Chief Justice submitted that it was the responsibility of those who wear the robes to keep our legal maxims in step with the "enlightened common sense" of the country. He continued: "Our judges are not monks or scientists, but participants in the living stream of our national life, steering the law between the dangers of rigidity on the one hand and of formlessness on the other. Legal scholars may still debate whether the life of the law is reason, as Coke maintained, or experience, as Holmes claimed. I think it is both. Our system faces no theoretical dilemma but a single continuous problem: how to apply to ever changing conditions the never changing principles of freedom." Regarding the place of the judiciary in the scheme of things, he held that while it had sometimes misused its prerogative of review, it had never done so to the point of deserving a forfeiture of that power. The court was kept in line with the other branches of government not only by the Constitution but by a custom of "self-restraint and impersonality."[19]

Certainly Warren has not always abided by the last part of his message or by the words of Paul Freund: "The art of being a justice is to achieve change without too great a loss in continuity —to preceive the direction in which society is moving, yet be prudent about the lengths to which the move is carried."[20] Still, no man of his temperament and background could be oblivious of such standards of behavior. And one cannot ignore very real,

---

[19] Earl Warren, "The Law and the Future," *Fortune*, 52, No. 5 (Nov., 1955), 107, 224.

[20] Quoted in Ernest Havemann, "Storm Center of Justice," *Life*, 56, No. 21 (May 22, 1964), 124.

if not too obvious, safeguards against sporadic lapses in judicial probity: the safety of numbers on the top bench, an inevitable erosion of ideas and philosophy with age and time (e.g., Frankfurter), and those changes in personnel that must come, as sure as fate, as the years pass. Furthermore, the constitutional and political structure of the United States has enough built-in strengths and protections to withstand periodic forays beyond what most people might consider prudent. In the meantime most Americans still expect, and their system envisages, an unbridled exercise of will by the justices in discharging their duties as they see them. As Havemann perceptively noted, there is a parallel here between the present tribunal and the first one, under John Marshall. That first tribunal was also given to aggressiveness and bold injunctions. It, too, ran into strong opposition. Yet it not only endured; it ultimately prevailed.

Bibliographic Notes

CHAPTER I, *Earl Warren: Political Practices and Political Principles*

There are numerous sources that sketch California's political system before, during, and following the governorship of Earl Warren. One fine text among many is Winston W. Crouch, Dean E. McHenry, John C. Bollens, and Stanley Scott, *California Government and Politics*, 4th ed. (Englewood Cliffs, N.J.: Prentice-Hall, 1967). More political in cast is the new volume by Richard B. Harvey, *The Dynamics of California Politics and Government* (Belmont: Wadsworth, 1969). See also Harvey's chapter entitled "California Politics: Historical Profile" in Eugene P. Dvorin and Arthur J. Misner, eds., *California Politics and Policies: Original Essays* (Palo Alto: Addison-Wesley, 1966), one of the leading books of readings on the subject.

A number of citations relate to specific features of the California political scene that shaped the political environment in which Warren operated. On the state's now defunct but then crucial cross-filing system consult, for example, Evelyn Hazen, *Cross-Filing in Primary Elections* (Berkeley: Univ. of California Press, 1951) or Robert J. Pitchell, "The Electoral System and Voting Behavior: The Case of California's Cross-Filing," *Western Political Quarterly*, XII, No. 2 (June, 1959), 459-84. On the functioning of local nonpartisanship, see the scholarly work by Eugene C. Lee, *The Politics of Nonpartisanship* (Berkeley: Univ. of California Press, 1960). Dated but relevant to the Warren period on the topic of direct legislation is Winston W. Crouch, *The Initiative and Referendum in California* (Los Angeles: Haynes Foundation, 1950). The same observation is true of Warren S. Thompson, *Growth and Changes in California's Population* (Los Angeles: Haynes Foundation, 1955). The state's diverse sectionalism is the concern of Ruth E. Baugh, "California: A Type Study of a State," *Education*, 69, No. 1 (Sept., 1948), 16-23.

The growth and activities of volunteer party bodies in California are treated in Hugh A. Bone, "New Party Associations in the West," *American Political Science Review*, XLV, No. 4 (Dec., 1951), 1115-25; Leonard C. Rowe, *Preprimary Endorsements in California Politics* (Berkeley: Univ. of California, Bureau of Public Administration, 1961); and Currin V. Shields, "A Note on Party Organization: The Democrats in California," *Western Political Quarterly*, VII, No. 4 (Dec., 1954), 673-83. The raw material on pressure groups and lobbying can be found in the releases of the various legislative committees on legislative representation; see *List of Legislative Advocates and Organizations* (Sacramento: issued periodically). A colorful, if somewhat exaggerated, account of the machinations of Artie Samish, "lobbyist extrordinaire" for the liquor industry in the Warren era, is in Lester Velie, "The Secret Boss of California," *Collier's*, 124, No. 7 (Aug. 13, 1949), 11-13, 71-73; No. 8 (Aug. 20, 1949), 12-13, 60, 62-63.

Insights into the functions and controversies surrounding California's famed political public relations firms can be had by examining such works as Stanley Kelley, *Professional Public Relations and Political Power* (Baltimore: Johns Hopkins Press, 1956); Carey McWilliams, "Government by Whitaker and Baxter," *Nation*, 172, No. 15 (Apr. 14, 1951), 346-48; No. 16 (Apr. 21, 1951), 366-69; No. 18 (May 5, 1951), 418-21; and Robert J. Pitchell, "The Influence of Professional Campaign Management Firms in Partisan Elections in California," *Western Political Quarterly*, XI, No. 2 (June, 1958), 278-300. Voting behavior in California spanning the Warren years is in Eugene C. Lee, *California Votes: 1928-1960* (Berkeley: Univ. of California, Institute of Governmental Studies, 1963).

For my information and ideas about Warren's political practices and principles, and their application to specific phases of politics and government in California, I placed heaviest reliance upon interviews with some thirty-eight officeholders and political activists from both major parties, friendly and unfriendly toward the former governor and chief justice, deeply involved in the state politics of that era or the Warren administration. These authorities were—

John S. Barcome (R), former chairman of Los Angeles County Republican Central Committee, former vice chairman of Republican State Central Committee, 1942 field chairman for Southern California Warren campaign organization (interview, Apr. 11, 1959)

Hon. Julian Beck (D), judge of Superior Court of Los Angeles County, former legislative secretary to Gov. Edmund G. Brown, former judge of Municipal Court of Los Angeles, former member of California State Assembly (interview, May 11, 1956)

Earl C. Behrens (R), then political editor of *San Francisco Chronicle* (interview, Jan. 24, 1957)

Bernard Brennan (R), Los Angeles lawyer, former chairman of Los Angeles County Republican Central Committee, Warren campaign manager for Southern California in 1946 (interview, Dec. 27, 1956)

Hon. Louis Burke (R), justice of California Supreme Court, former justice of California District Court of Appeals, former judge of Superior Court of Los Angeles County, vice chairman of 1950 Southern California Warren campaign organization (interview, Apr. 13, 1959)

Hon. J. Frank Coakley (R), district attorney of Alameda County and a former deputy to Warren in that office (interview, Mar. 13, 1958)

Hon. Charles J. Conrad (R), member of California State Assembly (interview, Dec. 31, 1956)

Thomas J. Cunningham (R), vice president and general counsel of University of California, former judge of Superior Court of Los Angeles County, former member of California State Assembly, 1946 campaign chairman for Warren in Southern California (letter to me, Apr. 29, 1959)

Hon. T. H. De Lap (deceased) (R), former Richmond, Cal., lawyer, former chairman of Republican State Central Committee, former state senator of Contra Costa County (letter, May 1, 1959)

Hon. Jess Dorsey (deceased) (R), former state senator of Kern County (interview, Mar. 4, 1958)

Wallace K. Downey (R), Los Angeles lawyer and former insurance commissioner under Gov. Warren (interview, Apr. 22, 1959)

Hon. McIntyre Faries (R), former judge of Superior Court of Los Angeles County, former vice chairman of Republican State Central Committee, former party national committeeman (interview, Apr. 8, 1959)

Cornelius J. Haggerty (D), president of Building and Construction Trades Department, A.F.L.-C.I.O., former secretary-treasurer of California State Federation of Labor (interview, May 22, 1956)

Gordon R. Hahn (R), former member of Los Angeles City Council, former member of California State Assembly (interview, Feb. 26, 1957)

Dr. Wilton L. Halverson (deceased) (R), former Los Angeles physician and former director of public health under Gov. Warren (interview, Apr. 9, 1959)

Victor R. Hansen (R), Los Angeles lawyer, former judge of Superior Court of Los Angeles County, former chief of Antitrust Division, U.S. Dept. of Justice, Southern California chairman for Warren in 1950 (interview, Apr. 23, 1959)

Hon. Augustus F. Hawkins (D), member of House of Representatives, former member of California State Assembly (interview, Dec. 27, 1956)

Kenneth Holland (D), Beverly Hills lawyer, member of 1950 Democrats for Warren Committee of Southern California (interview, Apr. 14, 1959)

Karl Holton (R), former probation officer of Los Angeles County, former director of California Youth Authority for Gov. Warren (interview, Apr. 14, 1959)

Hon. Frederick F. Houser (R), former member of California State Assembly, former lieutenant governor of California under the first Warren term, 1943-47; former judge of Superior Court of Los Angeles County (interview, Apr. 15, 1959)

Ralph Hoyt (R), former judge of Superior Court of Alameda County, former district attorney of that jurisdiction and a former deputy to District Atty. Warren (interview, Mar. 13, 1958)

Robert W. Kenny (D), judge of Superior Court of Los Angeles County, former attorney general of California, 1943-47; defeated by Warren for governor in 1946 (interview, Dec. 27, 1956)

Harold K. Levering (deceased) (R), former member of California State Assembly (interview, Feb. 14, 1957)

Thomas Maloney (deceased) (R), former member of California State Assembly and of California State Senate (interview, Jan. 22, 1957)

Richard A. McGee (R), former administrator of Youth and Adult Corrections Agency and former director of corrections under Warren (letter, June 10, 1959)

Lester A. McMillan (D), former member of California State Assembly (interview, May 17, 1956)

Rollin McNitt (D), Los Angeles lawyer, former chairman of Democratic Central Committee of Los Angeles County (interview, Apr. 18, 1959)

James Oakley (R), former judge of Superior Court of Sacramento County, former executive secretary to Gov. Warren, former deputy to District Atty. Warren in Alameda County, and former deputy attorney general to Warren (interview, Feb. 20, 1958)

Culbert L. Olson (deceased) (D), governor of California 1939-43, defeated by Warren in 1942 (interview, Jan. 3, 1958)

Herbert L. Phillips (D), then political editor of *Sacramento Bee* (interview, Jan. 24, 1957)

Verne Scoggins (R), former regional director, U.S. Post Office, San Francisco; former press secretary to Gov. Warren (interview, Mar. 14, 1958)

Edward S. Shattuck (deceased) (R), former chairman of Los Angeles County Republican Central Committee, former chairman of State Central Commtitee, former GOP national committeeman, Republican candidate for California attorney general in 1950 (interview, Apr. 15, 1959)

Hon. William T. Sweigert (D), U.S. district court judge, former judge of Superior Court of San Francisco County, former executive secretary to Gov. Warren, and former deputy to Atty. Gen. Warren (interview, Jan. 20, 1957)

Loren C. Vanderlip (R), former legislative representative for California State Chamber of Commerce (interview, Jan. 30, 1958)

Hon. Beach Vasey (R), judge of Superior Court of Los Angeles County, former legislative secretary to Gov. Warren (interview, May 3, 1956)

Laughlin E. Waters (R), Los Angeles lawyer, former U.S. attorney for Southern California; former member of California State Assembly (interview, Jan. 9, 1957)

Hon. Alfred Wollenberg (R), U.S. district court judge, former judge of Superior Court of San Francisco, former member of California State Assembly (interview, May 22, 1956)

Hon. Evelle J. Younger (R), district attorney of Los Angeles County, former judge of Los Angeles County Superior Court, former chairman of Los Angeles County Republican Central Committee (interview, Apr. 8, 1959)

Biographical treatments of Warren's life and career can be found in a number of books and articles. See, for example, the studies by Leo Katcher, *Earl Warren: A Political Biography* (New York: McGraw-Hill, 1967) and John D. Weaver, *Warren: The Man, The Court, The Era* (Boston: Little, Brown, 1967). Decidedly older and quite dated is the campaign tract by Irving Stone, *Earl Warren, A Great American Story* (New York: Prentice-Hall, 1948). Biographical sketches abound in popular journals. Most relevant to an overview of the governorship are Gordon Harrison, "Warren of California," *Harper's*, 204, No. 1225 (June, 1952), 27-32; Herbert L. Phillips, "Warren of California," *Nation*, 174, No. 21 (May 24, 1952), 495-97; and Beverly Smith, "Earl Warren's Greatest Moment," *Saturday Evening Post*, 227, No. 4 (July 24, 1954), 17-19, 48, 53. A most unflattering picture of the then freshman governor was painted by Carey McWilliams, "Warren of California," *New Republic*, 109 (Oct. 18, 1943), 514-17. Later summaries are in Ernest Havemann, "Storm Center of Justice," *Life*, 56, No. 21 (May 22, 1964), 108-10, 113-14, 116-18, 121-22, 124, and "The Warren Court: Fateful Decade," *Newsweek*, LXIII, No. 19 (May 11, 1964), 24-28, 33.

The publications above shed light on Warren's political beliefs during his days as California chief executive. His own expressions on party affairs, policy questions, and matters of governmental philosophy are contained in such pieces as "Building for the Future in the West," *State Government*, XIX (Jan., 1946), 3-5; "Victory, Lasting Peace, Jobs for All," keynote address to Republican National Convention, June 26, 1944, in *Vital Speeches of the Day*, X, No. 19 (July 15, 1944), 588-92; and "Quizzing Warren," an interview with Gov. Warren, *U.S. News & World Report*, XXXII, No. 18 (May 2, 1952), 38-47. A later collection of Warren's ideas and statements, although pertaining more to the high court than to the governorship, is in Henry M. Christman, ed., *The Public Papers of Chief Justice Earl Warren* (New York: Simon and Schuster, 1959).

Indispensable to me for data on the content of Warren's programs while he served in Sacramento, as well as for insights into his political approach, were the *Warren Speeches*, a collection located in the California Room, State Library, Sacramento. Most helpful also were the files of the *Los Angeles Times, Sacramento Bee,* and *San Francisco Chronicle.* While the *Times* has improved tremendously in that regard since Warren's time, the *Bee* then contained the most complete coverage of state politics and the Sacramento scene, particularly in the columns and news stories of its outstanding former political editor Herbert L. Phillips.

CHAPTER II, *"Earl Warren: The Political Campaigner"*

For background on campaign organization, finance, strategy, and tactics in the United States as a whole one can consult any of the better texts or other works that discuss American political parties and politics. Among the best are Hugh A. Bone, *American Politics and the Party System,* 3rd ed. (New York: McGraw-Hill, 1965); V. O. Key, *Politics, Parties and Pressure Groups,* 5th ed. (New York: Crowell, 1964); and Clinton Rossiter, *Parties and Politics in America* (Ithaca: Cornell Univ. Press, 1960). More specific to the subject is the treatise by Stanley Kelley, *Political Campaigning* (Washington: Brookings Institution, 1960). Also in point is Kelley's *Professional Public Relations and Political Power,* cited in Chapter I. Excellent analyses of the exciting Kennedy-Nixon presidential race in 1960 are in Paul T. David, ed., *The Presidential Election and Transition, 1960–61* (Washington: Brookings Institution, 1961). On campaign finance see Herbert E. Alexander, *Regulation of Political Finance* (Princeton: Citizens' Research Foundation, 1966) and Alexander Heard, *The Costs of Democracy* (Chapel Hill: Univ. of North Carolina Press, 1962).

For descriptions of the Warren campaign organizations and insights into his style of campaigning for the governorship I am particularly indebted to a number of the authorities listed in the previous chapter, specifically Barcome, Brennan, Burke, Conrad, Cunningham, Faries, Hahn, Hansen, Holland, Houser, McNitt, Scoggins, and Shattuck. Extensive use was also made of the *Warren Speeches* and the files of the *Sacramento Bee.* The Olson-Warren feud and the 1942 contest are highlighted in Robert E. Burke, *Olson's New Deal for California* (Berkeley: Univ. of California Press, 1953). Aspects of the strained relations between Warren and Nixon are in Earl Mazo, *Richard Nixon: A Political and Personal Portrait* (New York: Harper-Avon, 1960). Crucial to an understanding and interpretation of the sources and nature of Warren's campaign contributions and expenditures, however restricted, are the Statements of Campaign Receipts and Expenditures (titles vary) located in the archives of the office of secretary of state in Sacramento.

CHAPTER III, *"Earl Warren: Executive Policymaker"*

Although dated, a good overview of the role of American governors in the policymaking processes of the states (with some references to Earl Warren) is Coleman Ransone, *The Office of Governor in the United States* (Birmingham: Univ. of Alabama Press, 1956). Any good study of general state government will provide additional perspective. Outstanding in its stress on political dynamics is Duane Lockard, *The Politics of State and Local Government* (New York: Macmillan, 1963). Further information about the positions and problems of state chief executives within the administration, particularly relative to California, is available in James R. Bell and Earl L. Darrah, *State Executive Reorganization* (Berkeley: Univ. of California, Bureau of Public Administration 1961). The leading studies of the presidency help to clarify the part played by chief executives in developing governmental programs and furnish points of comparison and contrast with state governors on that subject. See, for example, Louis W. Koenig, *The Chief Executive* (New York: Harcourt, Brace, World, 1964) and Richard E. Neustadt, *Presidential Power: The Politics of Leadership* (New York: Wiley, 1960). Also in point here is Richard Fenno, *The President's Cabinet: An Analysis in the Period from Wilson to Eisenhower* (Boston: Harvard Univ. Press, 1959).

Again most valuable to me for enlightenment on program development and related features of the Warren administration were several of the authorities previously cited, namely Behrens, Downey, Haggerty, Halverson, Holton, Maloney, McGee, Oakley, Phillips, Sweigert, Vanderlip, and Vasey. A good source of data on the principal advisers to Warren and the procedures used in selecting them is James Bell, "The Executive Office of the California Governor under Earl Warren, 1943–1953" (unpublished Ph.D. dissertation, Univ. of California, Berkeley, 1956). Biographical data for the Warren appointees is in *California Blue Book* of 1942, 1946, 1950, and 1954. Particularly useful on the Governor's Council part way through Warren's tenure is the document by the California State Dept. of Finance, *Survey of the Governor's Council,* Report A.N. 120, July 25, 1947 (Sacramento: 1947). An excellent summary of the historical development and major issues of California's civil service system through the Warren period is in the State Personnel Board's *Twenty-first Biennial Report,* July 1, 1952–June 30, 1954 (Sacramento: 1954). Essential to the section on Warren's citizen advisory bodies were the many reports of the various conferences, committees, and commissions.

CHAPTER IV, *"Earl Warren: Legislative Advocate"*

The voluminous literature on the organization, procedures, politics, problems, and personalities of Congress is a valuable backdrop for comprehension of the legislative process. Perhaps the best of a very good lot is Daniel M. Berman, *In Congress Assembled: The Legislative Process in the National Government* (New York: Macmillan, 1964). Facets of executive-legislative relations are the concern of such works as Wilfred E. Binkley, *President and Congress* (New York: Vintage Press, 1962) and James M. Burns, *The Deadlock of Democracy: Four-Party Politics in America* (Englewood Cliffs, N.J.: Prentice-Hall, 1963). Dealing with American state legislatures are such scholarly works as Alexander Heard, ed., *State Legislatures in American Politics* (Englewood Cliffs, N.J.: Prentice-Hall, 1966); Malcolm E. Jewell, *The State Legislature: Politics and Practice* (New York: Random House, 1962); and John C. Wahlke, Heinz Eulau, William Buchanan, and Leroy C. Ferguson, *The Legislative System: Explorations in Legislative Behavior* (New York: Wiley, 1962). Bridging the gap between the two principal levels is William Keefe and Morris Ogul, *The American Legislative Process: Congress and the States* (Englewood Cliffs, N.J.: Prentice-Hall, 1964) and Malcolm E. Jewell and Samuel C. Patterson, *The Legislative Process in the United States* (New York: Random House, 1966).

Up-to-date and comprehensive works on California's legislature are few. The most recent, dealing also with the local level, is the well-written little volume by George S. Blair and Houston I. Flournoy, *Legislative Bodies in California* (Belmont, Cal.: Dickenson, 1967). Older works but presenting the major features are Joseph A. Beek, *The California Legislature* (Sacramento: 1957) and Arthur A. Ohnimus, *The Legislature of California* (Sacramento: 1962). The most scholarly investigation of the workings of the California legislature in recent history, in this instance with emphasis upon the interaction of partisan, group, and other related factors, is William Buchanan, *Legislative Partisanship: The Deviant Case of California* (Berkeley: Univ. of California Press, 1963). Of great assistance to me in analyzing voting patterns in California's assembly and senate during the Warren era were the various reports of the state Federation of Labor on both floor and committee actions, supplementing the official roll calls in the legislative journals. Of the authorities cited earlier, those of greatest aid in developing this chapter were Beck, Conrad, Dorsey, Hahn, Hawkins, Levering, Maloney, McMillan, Sweigert, Vasey, Waters, and Wollenberg.

CHAPTER V, *"Earl Warren: Program Innovator"*

The raw material on California's public health services during the Warren years is in *California Public Health Reports,* published by the State Dept. of Public Health, from July 1, 1943, through June 30, 1954. Pertinent to the Warren governorship as well as thereafter are such official documents as California Dept. of Public Health, *Health in California* (Sacramento: 1957); California Governor's Committee on Medical Aid and Health, *Health Care for California: A Report* (Berkeley: California Dept. of Public Health, 1960); and California Legislature, Assembly Interim Committee on Public Health, *Final Report to the Legislature* (Sacramento: 1951).

Vital statistical and descriptive data on California's mental hygiene operations during the Warren period is in *Biennial and Statistical Reports* of the state departments of Institutions and Mental Hygiene for the years ending June 30, 1943, through June 30, 1953. Additional statistical data, particularly valuable in comparing California's position in the field with that of other jurisdictions, is available in a number of federal government sources: U.S. Bureau of the Census, *Patients in Mental Institutions: 1943* (Washington: 1946); U.S. Department of Health, Education, and Welfare, Public Health Service, *Patients in Mental Institutions: 1950 and 1951* (Washington: 1954); and U.S. Federal Security Agency, Public Health Service, *Patients in Mental Institutions: 1949* (Washington: 1952). Quite valuable also were the final reports of the two governor's conferences called by Warren on mental health and senile patients: *Final Report of the Governor's Conference on the Care and Treatment of Senile Patients,* Sept. 14, 1950 (Sacramento: 1950) and *Final Report of the Governor's Conference on Mental Health,* Mar. 3 and 4, 1949 (Sacramento: 1949). Subsequent developments regarding some of the innovations launched by Warren can be found in California Dept. of Mental Hygiene, *Outpatient Psychiatric Clinics: 1962 California Resources* (Sacramento: 1963); Margaret Greenfield, *Providing for Mental Illness* (Berkeley: Univ. of California, Institute of Governmental Studies, 1964); and Margaret Greenfield, *State-Local Mental Health Services* (Berkeley: Univ. of California, Bureau of Public Administration, 1955).

Historical perspective on the battle for health insurance in California is obtainable from Paul A. Dodd and E. F. Penrose, *Economic Aspects of Medical Services, with Special Reference to Conditions in California* (Washington: Graphic Arts, 1939). Essential to an understanding of the issues and disputes concerning Warren's proposal is California Legislature,

Assembly Public Health Committee, *Compulsory Health Insurance*, Hearings on AB 449 and AB 800, 56th Sess., June 12, 1945 (Sacramento: 1945). The role of Whitaker and Baxter in the health insurance fight in California and in the subsequent national battle during the Truman administration is treated in Kelley, "Professional Public Relations," and McWilliams, "Government by Whitaker and Baxter," both previously cited.

Information on California's social welfare programs during the Warren administration is in *Biennial Reports* of state Dept. of Social Welfare from June 30, 1944, through June 30, 1954. A brief history of state activities in the area is given in the report for the biennium July 1, 1938, to June 30, 1940. Valuable also are the proceedings of the Chief Executive's 1951 conference on the aging, *Proceedings of the Governor's Conference on the Problems of the Aging*, Oct. 15 and 16, 1951 (Sacramento: 1951), as well as *Report of California's Mid-Century Conference on Children and Youth*, Sept. 18-19, 1950 (Sacramento: 1950). Further statistical data and California's ranking compared with other jurisdictions in different facets of public assistance is located in several federal documents: U.S. Dept. of Health, Educaton, and Welfare, Social Security Administration, *Social Security Bulletin, December 1953*, Vol. 16, No. 12 (Washington: 1953); U.S. Dept. of Health, Education, and Welfare, Social Security Administration, *Social Security Bulletin, September 1954*, Vol. 17, No. 9 (Washington: 1954); U.S. Federal Security Agency, Social Security Board, *Social Security Bulletin, March 1943*, Vol. 6, No. 3 (Washington: 1943); U.S. Federal Security Agency, Social Security Board, *Social Security Yearbook: 1943* (Washington: 1944); and U.S. Federal Security Agency, Social Security Board, *Social Security Yearbook: 1944* (Washington: 1945).

Material on other specific phases of California's welfare system during the Warren years is in numerous legislative committee reports. Representative are the following: California Legislature, Assembly Interim Committee on Social Welfare, *Final Report* (Sacramento: 1953); California Legislature, Senate Interim Committee on Social Welfare, *Needed Revisions in Social Welfare Legislation: Report* (Sacramento: 1951); *ibid.*, *Report* (Sacramento: 1949); *ibid.*, *Report* (Sacramento: 1951); *ibid.*, *Report*, May 1953 (Sacramento: 1953). Later investigations are those by the Commonwealth Club of California and undertaken by Vaughn D. Bornet, *California Social Welfare: Legislation, Financing, Services, Statistics* (Englewood Cliffs, N.J.: Prentice-Hall, 1956) and by the Welfare Study Commission, *Final Report* (Sacramento: 1963).

Pension politics in California, with special stress on the activities of George McLain, is the subject of several works. See, for example, Floyd A. Bond and others, *Our Needy Aged* (New York: Holt, 1954), which also sheds light on other facets of California's old age security program during the Warren governorship; Carey McWilliams, "Lobbyist for the Aged," *Frontier*, 2, No. 6 (Apr., 1951), 5-9; Carey McWilliams, "Pension Politics in California," *Nation*, 169, No. 14 (Oct. 1, 1949), 320-22; and Frank A. Pinner, Paul Jacobs, and Philip Selznick, *Old Age and Political Behavior* (Berkeley: Univ. of California Press, 1959), a book that deals almost exclusively with the McLain organization.

Essential to the question of employment planning in California during the Warren governorship are *Biennial Reports* of the state departments of Employment and Industrial Relations. Two other publications of the latter agency, *Handbook of Labor Statistics: 1951–1952* (San Francisco: 1953) and *Handbook of Labor Statistics: 1953–1954* (San Francisco: 1955), provide vital data on the results of employment planning and related topics. Financial information on Warren's reserve funds is pinpointed in *Annual Reports* of the state controller, that for the fiscal year ending June 30, 1953, being particularly relevant. Descriptions of employment programs are presented in *Proceedings of the Governor's Conference on Employment, Dec. 5-6, 1949* (Sacramento: Department of Employment, 1950); *Report and Recommendations of the California State Reconstruction and Re-Employment Commission*, period ending Dec. 31, 1944 (Sacramento: 1945); *Report and Recommendations of the California State Reconstruction and Re-Employment Commission*, year ending Dec. 31, 1945 (Sacramento: 1946); and *Third Report to the Governor and the Legislature of the California State Reconstruction and Re-Employment Commission* (Sacramento: 1947). The goals and early operations of the last-named agency are given in its document *Objectives, Organization, Program, March 1944* (Sacramento: 1944). One central phase of the full-employment issue during the Warren years is explained in the commission's release *A Production and Employment Estimate for California*, prepared by Van Beuren Stanbery, chief of technical staff, Oct. 16, 1945 (Sacramento: 1945).

Economic conditions and the task of finding jobs for a burgeoning population during the Warren period are subjects probed by Margaret S. Gordon, *Employment Expansion and Population Growth* (Berkeley: Univ. of California Press, 1954); Samuel C. May, *The Postwar Unemployment Problem in California, 1945–1947* (Berkeley: Univ. of California, Bureau of Public Administration, 1945); Davis McEntire, *The Labor Force in California* (Berkeley: Univ. of California Press, 1952); Alfred G. Morris, *The California Postwar Employment Problem* (Berkeley: Univ. of California, Bureau of Public Administration 1946); Earl Warren, "Building for the Future of the West," *State Government*, XIX, No. 1 (Jan., 1946), 3-5; Earl Warren (with Frank J. Taylor), "California's Biggest Headache," *Saturday Evening Post*, 221, No. 7 (Aug. 14, 1948), 20-21, 72, 74. Additional perspective on these matters since the Warren administration is available in Robert K. Arnold and others, *The California Economy: 1947–1980* (Menlo

Park: Stanford Research Institute, 1961); California Economic Development
Agency, *Current Economic Trends: The Nation and California* (Sacramento:
1960); California Legislature, Senate Fact-Finding Committee on Commerce and Economic Development, *Final Report* (Sacramento: 1959); and
Elizabeth Y. Deran, *Financing Capital Improvements: the "Pay-as-You Go"
Approach* (Berkeley: Univ. of California Press, 1961). Mediation activities
during the Warren administration are related in two bulletins of the California Conciliation Service, *The Adjustment of Labor Disputes* (San
Francisco: 1948 and 1951). Later and more comprehensive is the publication by the University of California, Institute of Industrial Relations, *Labor
and Labor Relations on the West Coast* (Berkeley: 1959).

California's system of unemployment benefits during much of the
Warren governorship is discussed in Arthur P. Allen, *Unemployment
Insurance in California* (Los Angeles: Haynes Foundation, 1950). Various
of its operations then are also probed in California Dept. of Employment,
A Sourcebook on Unemployment Insurance in California (Sacramento:
1953); California Legislature, Senate Interim Committee on Unemployment
Insurance, *Report* (Sacramento: 1945); and Michael T. Wermel, *Postwar
Changes in California Unemployment Insurance Experience* (Pasadena:
California Inst. of Technology, 1956). Features of this and other labor
benefit programs in California at the time are dealt with in the previously
cited reports of the Reconstruction and Re-Employment Commission, the
1949 employment conference, and the Dept. of Industrial Relations. The
Biennial Reports and *Handbook of Labor Statistics* of the last-named also
relate key financial data and other statistics on jobless insurance and workmen's compensation. See also Edward F. Staniford, *Recent State Labor
Legislation* (Berkeley: Univ. of California Press, 1949).

Crucial to a comparison of California with other jurisdictions in labor
benefits at the commencement and the termination of the Warren administration are a number of federal government documents: U.S. Bureau
of Employment Security, *Annual Report, Fiscal Year 1953* (Washington:
1954); U.S. Bureau of Employment Security, *Annual Report, Fiscal Year
1954* (Washington: 1955); U.S. Bureau of Employment Security, *Handbook on State Unemployment Compensation Laws: May 1942* (Washington: 1942); U.S. Bureau of Employment Security, "Handbook on State
Unemployment Insurance Laws," mimeographed, supplementary materials
to the 1942 *Handbook* (Washington: 1951); U.S. Bureau of Employment
Security, *Handbook of Unemployment Insurance, Financial Data, 1938–
1951,* mimeographed (Washington: 1952); U.S. Bureau of Labor Standards, *State Workmen's Compensation Laws, As of September 1954,* Bull.
No. 161 (Washington: 1955); U.S. Dept. of Labor, Division of Labor
Standards, *Workmen's Compensation: An Outline of Legislation in the
United States and Territories as of January 1, 1943,* Bull. No. 56 (Washing-

ton: 1943); and the *Social Security Bulletin, September 1954* and *Social Security Yearbook: 1944*, cited previously.

The question of unemployment insurance coverage for agricultural workers during the Warren years is considered in California Legislature, Joint Committee on Agriculture and Livestock Problems, *The Recruitment and Placement of Farm Laborers in California, 1950, with Special Consideration and Recommendation Concerning Proposals for Extension of Unemployment Insurance*, Special and Partial Report (Sacramento: 1951). More current on the state's continuing farm labor problems is the comprehensive California Legislature, Senate Fact-Finding Committee on Labor and Welfare, *Hearings on Farm Labor Problems* (Sacramento: 1959-60). Developments in jobless compensation subsequent to the Warren governorship are in Michael T. Wermel and Carl G. Uhr, *Financial Prospects for the California Unemployment Insurance Program in the 1960's: A Report to the Senate Committee on Insurance and Financial Institutions* (Sacramento: 1961).

The following are relevant to the industrial-accident program in California when Warren was in Sacramento: California Legislature, Assembly Interim Committee on Finance and Insurance, *First Preliminary Report on Workmen's Compensation Insurance* (Sacramento: 1950); California Legislature, Senate Interim Committee on Workmen's Compensation Benefits, *Partial Report* (Sacramento: 1951); *ibid., Report* (Sacramento: 1953); Warren L. Hanna, *The Law of Employee Injuries and Workmen's Compensation* (Albany, Cal.: Hanna Legal Publications, 1953). More recent is Hanna's *Workmen's Compensation Laws of California* (New York: Bender, 1963).

The issue of discrimination in employment during Warren's administration is dealt with in John T. Berry, "Fair Employment Practices in California: A Study of the Groups and Pressures Influencing Opinion on This Issue" (unpublished M.A. thesis, Univ. of California, Berkeley, 1952). More up to date are the various reports of California's Fair Employment Practices Commission.

The thinking of California's major labor organization concerning the different programs and services for the workingman during Warren's tenure as state chief executive is contained in the *Officers' Reports and Proceedings* of the annual conventions of the California State Federation of Labor. Also most helpful to me was California Labor League for Political Education, "Summary of Governor Warren's Legislative Record, 1943–1949," mimeographed, and located in the group's headquarters in San Francisco.

Quite valuable for the construction results of the Warren governorship in the fields of health, welfare, and labor, as well as in other areas, is the privately printed pamphlet written by a former press secretary to the Chief Executive, Verne Scoggins, *It Happened in California*, (Sept. 1,

1953). Necessary to an appreciation of the particular partisan overtones of public policies in these fields are the state and national platforms of the Democratic and Republican parties. Copies of those for California are in my possession; those for the national parties are conveniently reprinted in Kirk H. Porter and Donald B. Johnson, comps., *National Party Platforms, 1840–1956* (Urbana: Univ. of Illinois Press, 1956). Later editions of this publication also exist.

CHAPTER VI, *"Earl Warren, Social Progress, and Republicanism"*

Literature on the nature and function of American political parties is voluminous. The works by Bone, Key, and Rossiter, cited in Chapter II, on campaigns, are among the best sources for consultation. More behavioral in cast is Samuel J. Eldersveld, *Political Parties: A Behavioral Analysis* (Chicago: Rand McNally, 1964). A leading book of readings is by Frank Munger and Douglas Price, eds., *Readings in Political Parties and Pressure Groups* (New York: Crowell, 1964), as is John R. Owens and B. J. Staudenraus, eds., *The American Party System: A Book of Readings* (New York: Macmillan, 1965). More specific to each major party are Ralph M. Goldman, *The Democratic Party in American Politics* (New York: Macmillan, 1966) and Charles O. Jones, *The Republican Party in American Politics* (New York: Macmillan, 1965).

The sources cited in Chapter I regarding Warren's political beliefs are in point here—his own writings, those of others, and the interview material. The interviews most valuable to me were those with Beck, Brennan, Kenny, Levering, Oakley, Olson, Phillips, and Younger.

CHAPTER VII, *"Mr. Chief Justice"*

There is a profusion of books and articles on the role of the United States Supreme Court in the governmental process and its place in American history. A few principal titles are Henry J. Abraham, *The Judiciary: The Supreme Court in the Governmental Process* (Boston: Allyn, Bacon, 1965); Samuel Krislov, *The Supreme Court in the Political Process* (New York: Macmillan, 1965); Alpheus T. Mason, *The Supreme Court from Taft to Warren* (Baton Rouge: Louisiana State Univ. Press, 1958); and Leo Pfeffer, *This Honorable Court: A History of the United States Supreme*

Court (Boston: Beacon Press, 1965). Aspects of judicial behavior on the tribunal are the subject of an increasing number of publications. Three fine works by Glendon A. Schubert are (as editor) *Judicial Behavior: A Reader in Theory and Practice* (Chicago: Rand McNally, 1946), *Judicial Decision-Making* (Glencoe, Ill.: Free Press, 1963) and *The Judicial Mind: Attitudes and Ideologies of Supreme Court Justices, 1946–63* (Evanston, Ill.: Northwestern Univ. Press, 1965).

Many studies treat the judiciary or judicial process generally, such as Herbert Jacob, *Justice in America: Courts, Lawyers, and the Judicial Process* (Boston: Little, Brown, 1965); Walter F. Murphy and C. Herman Pritchett, eds., *Courts, Judges, and Politics: An Introduction to the Judicial Process* (New York: Random House, 1961); and Glendon A. Schubert, *Judicial Policy-Making: The Political Role of the Courts* (Chicago: Scott, Foresman, 1965).

Problems of judicial selection and phases of internal operation on the nation's top bench are probed by David J. Danelski, *A Supreme Court Justice is Appointed* (New York: Random House, 1964); Joel B. Grossman, *Lawyers and Judges: The A.B.A. and the Politics of Judicial Selection* (New York: Wiley, 1965); John R. Schmidhauser, *The Supreme Court: Its Politics, Personalities, and Procedures* (New York: Holt, Rinehart, Winston, 1960); and Alan F. Westin, ed., *The Supreme Court: Views from Inside* (New York: Norton, 1961). A more detailed look at the business of the high tribunal can be had from the annual analysis of its work by Paul C. Bartholomew, "The Supreme Court of the United States . . .", in the December issue of *Western Political Quarterly*, and from the yearly publication of the University of Chicago Press, *The Supreme Court Review*. Far too numerous to elaborate here are the biographical studies of supreme court justices that also enlighten on the role and activities of the tribunal. In point here is John P. Frank, *The Warren Court* (New York: Macmillan, 1964).

The many sources that have as their topics the protection of civil liberties and the exercise of basic freedoms in America include Twiley W. Barker, *Freedoms, Courts, Politics: Studies in Civil Liberties* (Englewood Cliffs, N.J.: Prentice-Hall, 1965); Osmond K. Fraenkel, *The Supreme Court and Civil Liberties* (New York: Oceana, 1960); Milton R. Konvitz, ed., *Bill of Rights Reader: Leading Constitutional Cases*, 2nd ed. (Ithaca: Cornell Univ. Press, 1960); Leo Pfeffer, *The Liberties of an American: The Supreme Court Speaks* (Boston: Beacon Press, 1963); and Rocco J. Tresolini, *Justice and the Supreme Court* (Philadelphia: Lippincott, 1963). The loyalty-security question and its relationship to the Warren court is examined in C. Herman Pritchett, *The Political Offender and the Warren Court* (Boston: Boston Univ. Press, 1958). Trial procedures and problems confronting the accused are in David Fellman, *The Defendant's Rights*

(New York: Rinehart, 1958) and Anthony Lewis, *Gideon's Trumpet* (New York: Random House, 1964).

Grandiose and growing is the literature on the subject of racial discrimination and the effects of recent Supreme Court decisions in that field. Consult, for example, Wallace Mendelson, *Discrimination* (Englewood Cliffs, N.J.: Prentice-Hall, 1962); Jack W. Peltason, *Fifty-eight Lonely Men: Southern Federal Judges and School Desegregation* (New York: Harcourt, Brace, World, 1961); Joseph Tussman, *The Supreme Court on Racial Discrimination* (New York: Oxford Univ. Press, 1963); and U.S. Commission on Civil Rights, *Annual Reports* and *Equal Protection of the Laws in Education* (Washington: 1961). A scholarly inquiry into the impact of Supreme Court decisions in the areas of both race and religion, as well as of reapportionment, is Alan P. Grimes, *Equality in America: Religion, Race and the Urban Majority* (New York: Oxford Univ. Press, 1964). Delving into constitutional issues of church and state are Philip B. Kurland, *Religion and the Law: Of Church and State and the Supreme Court* (Chicago: Aldin, 1962), and Joseph Tussman, *The Supreme Court on Church and State* (New York: Oxford Univ. Press, 1962). A multitude of books and articles deal with the reapportionment question and the high court's impact in that field. A leading source is Gordon E. Baker, *The Reapportionment Revolution: Representation, Political Power, and the Supreme Court* (New York: Random House, 1966). Relevant to the question of citizenship and expatriation and its consideration by America's top bench is John P. Roche, "The Expatriation Decisions: A Study in Constitutional Improvisations and the Uses of History," *American Political Science Review*, LVIII, No. 1 (Mar. 1964), 72-80.

In developing the thoughts and activities of Earl Warren as chief justice of the United States, I placed heaviest reliance on the following: Alexander M. Bickel, *Politics and the Warren Court* (New York: Harper, Row, 1965); the work edited by Henry Christman on Warren's public papers, the book by Frank on the Warren court, the article by Havemann in *Life*, the *Newsweek* article on "The Warren Court: Fateful Decade," all cited previously; Sam Kagel and Virginia Smith, "Chief Justice Warren and Labor Law," *California Law Review*, 49, No. 1 (Mar. 1961), 126-43; Pfeffer, "This Honorable Court," *supra*; Bernard Schwartz, " 'Warren Court'—An Opinion," *New York Times Magazine*, June 30, 1957, pp. 10-11; Earl Warren, "The Bill of Rights and the Military," *New York University Law Review*, 37, No. 2 (Apr., 1962), 181-203; Earl Warren, "The Law and the Future," *Fortune*, 52, No. 5 (Nov., 1955), 106-7, 224, 226, 229-30.

A number of other books and articles pertain to the pattern of decisions by the Warren court and the controversies it has generated in different fields of public policy. Illustrative are Ira M. Heyman, "The Chief Justice, Racial Segregation, and the Friendly Critics," *California Law Review*, 49,

No. 1 (Mar. 1961), 104-25; Clyde E. Jacobs, "The Warren Court—After Three Terms," *Western Political Quarterly*, IX, No. 4 (Dec., 1956), 937-54; Pritchett, "Political Offender and the Warren Court," *supra;* Harold J. Spaeth, "An Analysis of Judicial Attitudes in the Labor Relations Decisions of the Warren Court," *Journal of Politics*, 25, No. 2 (Mar., 1963), 290-311; Robert J. Steamer, "Statesmanship or Craftsmanship: Current Conflict over the Supreme Court," *Western Political Quarterly*, XI, No. 2 (June, 1958), 265-77; and J. Patrick White, "Warren Court Under Attack: The Role of the Judiciary in a Democratic Society," *Maryland Law Review*, XIX, No. 3 (Summer, 1959), 181-99. The following theses are also relevant: Walter Burnham, "Civil Liberties and the Dilemma of Judicial Power: The Warren Court and its Publics, 1953–1961" (unpublished Ph.D. dissertation, Harvard Univ., 1962); Clifford Lytle, "The Warren Court and its Political Critics" (unpublished Ph.D dissertation, Univ. of Pittsburgh, 1964); Theodore Vestal, "The Warren Court and Civil Liberties" (unpublished law dissertation, Stanford Univ., 1962).

Sour notes sounded about the Warren court, and the Chief Justice in particular, are numerous. One of the better-known of the right-wing polemics is Rosalie Gordon, *Nine Men Against America* (New York: Devon-Adair, 1958).